A PHOTO

# SNAKES
## AND OTHER REPTILES OF
# INDIA

### INDRANEIL DAS

Om Books International

This edition published in 2008 by Om Books International
4379/4B Prakash House, Ansari Road, Darya Ganj
New Delhi 110 002, India
Tel: +91-11-23263363, 23265303
Fax: +91-11-23278091
Email: sales@ombooks.com
www.ombooks.com

Copyright © 2002 in text: Indraneil Das
Copyright © 2002 in photographs: Indraneil Das (except individual photographers as credited)
Copyright © 2002, 2008 New Holland Publishers (UK) Ltd
Garfield House, 86–88 Edgware, London W2 2EA, UK
80 McKenzie Street, Cape Town 8001, South Africa
Unit 1, 66 Gibbes Street, Chatswood, NSW 2067, Australia
218 Lake Road, Northcote, Auckland, New Zealand
www.newhollandpublishers.com

ISBN 81 87108 35 5

Publishing Manager: Jo Hemmings
Project editor: Camilla MacWhannell
Edited and designed by D & N Publishing, Marlborough, Wiltshire
Cartography: Carte Blanche, Paignton, Devon
Production controller: Joan Woodroffe

Reproduction by Modern Age Repro House Limited, Hong Kong
Printed and bound in Malaysia by Times Offset (M) Sdn Bhd

10 9 8 7 6 5 4 3 2 1

All photos, including cover and title page, by the author.
Front cover photograph: Indian Trinket Snake.
Back cover photograph: Kuhl's Gliding Gecko.
Title page photograph: Spectacled Cobra.

**Acknowledgements**
I would like to thank the Universiti Malaysia Sarawak and the Centre for Herpetology, Madras Crocodile Bank Trust, for supporting the preparation of this photoguide. For the use of photographs, I would like to thank Steven Clement Anderson, Vivek Gour Broom, Ashok Sohrab Captain/The Lisus, Shekar Dattatri, Hla Tun, Ulrich Joger, David Thomas Jones, Michael Wai-Neng Lau, Harvey B. Lillywhite, Dong Lin, Matthias Lorenz, Shomen Mukherjee, Nikolai Lyuzianovich Orlov, Mark O'Shea, Samraat Pawar, S. U. Saravanakumar, Howard Bradley Shaffer, Joseph Bruno Slowinski, Frank Tillack, Peter Paul van Dijk, Miguel Vences, Gernot Vogel, Raju Vyas, Wolfgang Wüster and George Robert Zug. Finally, I thank Kraig Adler, Harry Andrews, Aaron Bauer, Patrick David, Anslem De Silva, Allen Greer, Rohan Pethiyagoda, Saibal Sengupta and Rom Whitaker for making available publications, aiding field work or generally providing support for the preparation of this work.

# Contents

Introduction. . . . . . . . . . . . . . . . . . . . . . . 4
About this book . . . . . . . . . . . . . . . . . . . 6
Reptile habitats in India . . . . . . . . . . . . . . 6
Conservation of reptiles . . . . . . . . . . . . . 9
Snake-bite and its management . . . . . . . 10
Species descriptions . . . . . . . . . . . . . . . . 12
Glossary. . . . . . . . . . . . . . . . . . . . . . . . 140
Further reading. . . . . . . . . . . . . . . . . . .141
Index . . . . . . . . . . . . . . . . . . . . . . . . . . 142

# Introduction

Loved or loathed by humans, snakes and other reptiles have had a special relationship with the people of India through the ages. While many snakes, turtles and crocodiles are revered, being considered as the vehicles of one of many hundred Hindu gods, or whether for more pragmatic reasons (e.g. as protectors of grain through their predation of rodent pests), large numbers of snakes and monitor lizards continue to be removed from the wild for the – now illegal – reptile skin industry. At the same time, the information available for conservation action is rather limited, the diverse habitats and ecological zones represented here remain poorly inventoried, and the natural history of all but the commonest species remains unknown.

India has almost 200 years of history in studies of herpetology – the science of the study of amphibians and reptiles – dating from the arrival of the erstwhile British East India Company. Active research has been conducted on the Indian peninsula itself, and the Indian reptile fauna is amongst the richest in the world, with a large number of endemic species and genera, as well as spectacular forms that delight the eye.

Although snakes are characterized by having neither limbs nor eyelids, several lizards share one of these characteristics, and the origin of snakes lies with lizards. Snakes are primarily predators of vertebrate animals, although a number of species specialize in invertebrates. As efficient hunters, prey are located by sight, as well as via chemical cues, which are collected with the aid of their bifid tongues and carried forward to a special sensory organ, located in the roof of the mouth, called the Jacobson's organ. Pit vipers and pythons, in addition to this oral organ, have thermal receptors on or near their lips, which permit them to detect the body heat of warm-blooded prey in darkness. Specialization of front (and in some cases, rear) teeth is shown by snakes of several groups, enabling the delivery of venom. The hollow, hypodermic needle-like fangs of the vipers are the most advanced type, while in cobras and kraits, the venom trickles down grooves into the prey body. Snakes inhabit virtually all types of habitat in the region, excluding the snow-clad peaks, although several species live on the edge of the snow-line, hibernating during the winter.

Lizards are generally recognizable from their close cousins, the snakes, in showing limbs, although a number of skinks have lost their limbs, thereby showing evolutionary convergence with snakes. Most lizards feed on insects or other invertebrates; adult monitor lizards are capable of subduing and eating small to medium-sized vertebrates, including birds and mammals. No Indian lizard is known to be venomous, and reports of food poisoning by lizards should be attributed to the unhygienic conditions under which the food was prepared. Several groups of lizards, including skinks, geckos and glass snakes, are capable of autotomizing their tails, that is, when threatened, they can willingly shed their tails, growing a new one later. However, the regenerated tail is never the same as the one that was lost, generally lacking the ornamentation and colour of the original tail.

Three species of crocodilians occur in India. They are heavily built, water-dwelling species, bearing large scales and large heads. Males tend to exceed females in size and all species feed on animals, ranging in size from fish to large mammals, depending on the size of the crocodile. The unique Gharial feeds exclusively on fish, having an extremely narrow snout to aid their capture. Crocodiles can be either hole-nesters, such as the Gharial and the Mugger, or mound-nesters, such as the Saltwater Crocodile, which rakes in leaves and mud from the bank to create a raised mound, inside which it deposits its eggs.

Turtles and tortoises complete the reptile fauna of India. India is home to over 30 marine, freshwater and terrestrial species, many of which are found exclusively in this country. The Olive Ridley Sea Turtle, which nests annually on the eastern coast of the country, forms the densest animal aggregation known, with tens of thousands nesting at the same time. Freshwater turtles are a favourite food item in eastern India, and are eagerly sought after. Therefore they are common only where they are not hunted, for example shrines along rivers, where communal basking by groups of up to a dozen turtles can be seen. Most of India's tortoise species are found only in

The external boundaries of India on this map have not been authenticated and may not be correct.

undisturbed hill forests, an exception being the Indian Star Tortoise, which is a member of the scrub community and semi-desert regions.

## About this book

At present, approximately 490 species have been recorded within the political boundaries of the Republic of India (including the islands of Andaman and Nicobars). This photographic guide describes and illustrates 243 of these (110 snakes; 98 lizards; 3 crocodilians; and 32 turtles and tortoises), including the more abundant and many otherwise distinctive species of snakes, lizards, crocodiles and turtles that one is likely to encounter, representing many genera. For every species covered, there is a brief description and a summary of known biology of the species, in addition to one or more colour photographs.

Each species account comprises a recommended English name, current scientific name, a brief description and a summary of its biology and distribution within India and outside the country. The length given is the maximum recorded for the individual species – snout-vent length for snakes, lizards and crocodilians, straight carapace length for turtles and tortoises. Listing of species is by groups (snakes, followed by lizards, crocodiles and turtles), and within these, by families, genera and species, in alphabetical order. Identifying species may be carried out by finding the appropriate picture to match a particular species, and confirming the identification from the morphological description and coloration, as well as distribution and biology, as provided in the text. A word of caution: this work does not pretend to be comprehensive and, therefore, specialist readers may wish to confirm identification with more technical works on the subject (listed towards the end of book, as well as others listed therein). The Indian herpetofauna remains poorly known, and many species remain undescribed by science.

## Reptile habitats in India

Reptile habitats in India, with a land area of 3,060,500 sq km, range from the high Himalayas to tropical forests, from shifting sand dunes to mangrove swamps and from seashores to urban centres. As expected, most of the reptile biodiversity of the region is to be found in undisturbed habitats. However, even for city dwellers, there is a great variety of species of lizards, snakes and even turtles that dwell within or close to larger cities, including shiny skinks in parks and gardens, the ubiquitous Garden Lizard, sometimes erroneously called 'Blood-sucker', worm snakes that sometimes invade our homes, through water inlets and the humble house gecko, of several species, found in nearly every house in the plains.

The country is under the influence of the monsoons, winds that blow during the summer and winter, producing large quantities of seasonal rainfall. While the rest of the country receives a single monsoon (the south-west), after the long and hot summer months, the south-east coast receives two, during the all too brief winter. Most reptilian activity in these areas is synchronized with rainfall: species time their activities, especially reproduction, with this period, to ensure abundant food supply for the young. At higher altitudes, reptiles are active during the summer months, hibernating during the cold weather. An understanding of local weather conditions is therefore of great importance to those seeking reptiles in this vast country.

The types of forest represented in India vary tremendously, a result of geological and other environmental factors and, in the last 10,000 years, much of the country's original forests have been lost to human activities, such as agriculture and urbanization. This has resulted in a loss of habitat for many forest-dwelling species, although a number of reptiles have managed to carve out niches for themselves in the altered habitats.

Brief descriptions of some of the ecological regions in the country are given below.

## Himalayas

The Himalayan range, stretching from Kashmir to Arunachal Pradesh, includes some of the highest mountains on earth, and has a major influence on the climate of the whole country. Vegetation types represented include moist deciduous, subtropical broad-leaved, coniferous forests and alpine grasslands and scrub forests, the foothills showing unique vegetation/physiography, such as the Terai (a swampy belt), Bhabar (with deep boulder deposits) and Duns (broad elevated valleys at $c.600$m). Geologically, the range is rather recent, although it has a large number of endemic genera and species of reptiles.

## Trans-Himalayas

The outer Himalayas includes the Zanskar, Ladakh and Karakorum, at the edge of the Tibetan Plateau. Located here is the largest glacier outside of the polar region, Siachen, 1,180km$^2$ in extent. The region is characterized by mountains that reach 6,600m, and the area includes subtropical evergreen forests at the lower elevations, and coniferous forests and steppes.

## Western Ghats

The hill range running along the west coast of the Deccan, or Peninsular India, referred to as the Western Ghats, is one of the 10 regions of greatest global biodiversity. A series of hill ranges, sometimes isolated by flat savannah, this region contains the highest mountains in the peninsula, reaching 2,695m in the Nilgiris, and annual precipitation exceeds 5,000mm. Vegetation types represented here include moist evergreen forests. The Western Ghats is home to a highly distinctive reptile fauna.

## Eastern Ghats

The hill range that runs along the east coast of India is the poor sister of the Western Ghats in terms of exploration and study. A weathered relic of the peninsular plateau, it comprises a series of isolated hills, reaching 1,750m at the Biligirirangan Hills, in the south. Several major rivers, including the Godavary, Mahanadi and Krishna, are responsible for breaks in the range. The dominant forest type is dry deciduous, although patches of moist deciduous and semi-evergreen forest also occur.

## Deccan

The reliefless Indian Peninsula, excluding the hill ranges on either side, is an extremely arid region. The vegetation here includes dry and moist deciduous forests. The Deccan has a rich, albeit poorly-known, reptile fauna, with a large number of species also occurring in adjacent regions, especially the North-west and the Eastern Ghats.

## North-east

The wettest region within India is the North-east, in the southern hills of the Himalayas. Rainfall exceeds 2,000mm and the region includes the wettest spot on earth (Mawsynram, in the Khasi Hills of Meghalaya State). The dominant vegetation types include moist deciduous, semi-evergreen and temperate montane forests. Trees loom to about 46m and vegetational complexity is one reason for the high herpetological diversity.

## North-west

The arid region to the north-west of India is similar in climate and vegetation to that of adjacent Pakistan. Bounded by the Indus and Nara Valleys in the west and the Aravali Range to the east, it includes the 446,000km$^2$ Thar Desert of Rajasthan. Approximately 6,000 years ago, the Indus Valley Civilization flourished here, at a time when the climate was more moist. The area is characterized by hills, stony plateaus, scrub and desert. This is the driest region of India, having on annual rainfall which is sometimes under 250mm.

## Bay Islands

The islands of the Andaman and Nicobars are historically part of the Republic of India (Port Blair, the administrative capital, served as a penal colony during the time of British rule). In terms of flora and fauna, they show an affinity to south-east Asia. Geologically, the Andamans are part of the Arakan mountains, detached by a rise in sea levels (except the volcanic island of Barren), while the Nicobars are a group of islands that sit on banks, and are of coralline origin. The range of vegetation represented in this archipelago of around 400 islands includes mangroves and wet evergreen forests.

# Conservation of reptiles

Apart from roughly a dozen species that are relatively flexible in terms of their habitat requirements (and which are therefore widespread, many being abundant in human-altered habitats), most of the species of reptiles in India are restricted to forested habitats of some sort. The greatest diversity is within the primary evergreen forests of north-eastern India, the Himalayan foothills, the Western Ghats and the Andaman and Nicobar Islands, all of which face serious threats from logging, damming, urbanization and mining. The removal of tree cover is devastating for many populations adapted to forest life.

Several species, perceived as dangerous, such as crocodiles and snakes, are killed out of fear and ignorance. There are no statistics on the numbers of snakes killed for this reason, but most of them belong to the category of large-growing, rat-eating species that are widespread in villages and rice fields.

Highways that pass through forested areas, for instance, are also known to be deadly for many reptile species that regularly attempt to cross, either to forage or as part of their seasonal migration.

Other reptiles are collected in large numbers for food or medicine. The freshwater turtle markets in eastern India used to display for sale as many as a dozen species; however, thanks to widespread publicity on their threatened status and the vigilance of enforcement officers, these have mostly disappeared. During the heyday of this trade, the commonest turtles were large softshell turtles with a high meat to bone ratio and a palatable flesh, such as the Indian Softshell Turtle and the Indian Flapshell Turtle. Turtles were caught all over the country to supply the markets of eastern India, probably causing an enormous drain on populations throughout the region.

Small numbers of turtles are still smuggled out of the country, and it is thought that their eventual destination is the markets of China. Local medicinal demand for reptiles concentrates on a few species – the Indian Spiny-tailed Lizard and the Indian Sandfish and, occasionally, one or more species of monitor lizards.

One growing market which exists is the pet trade, leading to many turtles, both aquatic and terrestrial, being collected from the wild. Many are illegally exported, both to the west and to the east. The Indian Star Tortoise is in great demand, as it has an attractive shell pattern, especially while juvenile; thousands are harvested annually. The Indian Roofed Turtle is a freshwater turtle avidly sought by the pet trade. Unfortunately, many of the eventual keepers of these turtles are young people, who have little experience in keeping such animals, and mortality is generally high.

All reptile species are protected in India, through listing in the country's wildlife conservation legislation. An important aspect of their conservation is the designation of a large number of protected areas, such as National Parks, Wildlife Sanctuaries and Reserve Forests, which are home to many species of reptiles.

# Snake-bite and its management

India is home to a large number of venomous snakes, several of which are found in the vicinity of human settlements, especially in rural areas, and in agricultural areas, where rats are in abundance. As a result, the number of deaths from snake-bites in India, estimated to be between 20,000 and 40,000 per year, is among the highest in the world. In this section are some precautionary measures for those who either deal with venomous reptiles in a professional capacity, who are interested in them as natural historians, or who simply encounter them while in the field.

Because there are fewer venomous snakes – at least those that are deadly – compared to non-venomous ones, it is generally possible to identify them. Vipers are relatively slow-moving snakes, with narrow necks and fat heads. Their fangs are folded when not in use. Cobras are large, heavy-bodied snakes that may raise a hood. They have short, fixed fangs. Coral snakes and kraits belong to the same family as the cobra, but cannot raise their hoods. Sea snakes are large, slender-bodied snakes with flat-tails that are always marine or at least coastal in distribution, although some might travel some considerable distance upriver. The sea kraits come on land, and can, in fact, even climb trees. They have short, fixed fangs. A word of caution: several non-venomous snakes mimic dangerous snakes, and the reverse is also true! Many snakes (such as the cat snakes and keelbacks) that do not bear true venom glands can nonetheless inflict painful bites, sometimes aided by a chewing motion, that might lead to complications.

When in the field, avoid putting your hand inside cracks or holes which might conceal a snake. In forests, wear shoes that completely cover the feet, and always carry a reliable torch. Headlamps (similar to the type used by miners, but now available in lightweight versions from camping goods companies) are even better – they allow both hands to be free. When crossing a fallen tree, look carefully under the tree on both sides (particularly the blind side). Keep houses and their surroundings free of garbage and litter, as these attract rats, which, in turn, attract snakes.

When handling a snake for study or photography, use a restrainer, such as a snake hook (typically an L-shaped stick) or better still, a snake-grabber. Store live snakes in cloth bags; check for holes and other weaknesses along the seams. If you are keeping snakes live in aquaria or terraria, ensure that the lid is secure. Landscape the enclosure, with plenty of places for concealment (such as bits of bark and vegetation, as well as rocks) and provide drinking water for snakes being otherwise kept dry. Avoid keeping venomous or unknown snakes: remember that they pose a hazard not only to you, but also to your family and neighbours.

The anti-venom serum commonly available in India is of the polyvalent type (made from the venom of the 'Big Four' – the Spectacled Cobra, Common Krait, Russell's Viper and Saw-scaled Viper), and is available in most primary health centres and hospitals. As most bites occur in rural or coastal areas, the patient needs to be reassured, kept warm, the region of the bite immobilized via a crepe (or any other stiff cloth) bandage and taken to a hospital as quickly as possible, if need be, by being carried. In cases where the patient has breathing difficulties, for example following envenoming by cobras and kraits, artificial respiration may be required. It is helpful in the treatment of the patient if an accurate description of the snake is provided. Do not cut or suck the wound, as this is likely to complicate the treatment as well as the subsequent healing process.

In the unlikely event of a snake-bite, remember that no snake in India can kill a healthy adult human being instantaneously and, if treated appropriately, most patients make a complete recovery.

# ACROCHORDIDAE (WART SNAKES)

Wart Snakes are stout, wrinkly-skinned aquatic snakes from the coastal waters of tropical Asia and Australasia. There are 3 species in the Asia-Pacific region, one of which occurs in India. All feed on fish. Sometimes wart snakes are killed for their skin or by coastal dwellers because of their fish-eating habit.

**Wart Snake** *Acrochordus granulatus* 1.00m

A heavy-bodied aquatic snake from the sea coasts as well as mangrove swamps. Head short and blunt, covered with granular scales; nostril valve-like, situated on top of snout; tail compressed laterally, ending in a point; skin with numerous small scales; head dark grey or black, body with alternating grey and cream bands, tapering towards the venter. A sluggish, non-aggressive snake, capable of remaining submerged underwater for over two hours. Nocturnal and found in mangrove swamps, mudflats and shallow coastal waters, sometimes entering rivers. Fish, primarily gobies and their relatives, form the diet of these snakes, although crustaceans are also consumed. Ovoviviparous, with clutches comprising 4–12 young that are produced in April, the newborn measuring 23cm. Found along both coasts of India, although apparently it is more abundant on the west coast. Also, Sri Lanka and Bangladesh, east to south-east Asia.

Harvey B. Lillywhite

# BOIDAE (BOAS AND PYTHONS)

The family of constricting snakes is represented in India by sand boas and pythons. They are stout-bodied snakes that lie in ambush for their prey, warm-bodied mammals and birds. Nearly all species from the region are threatened by the skin trade, and at least two of the Indian sand boas are in demand from snake charmers, being dramatic in appearance and hardy in captivity.

The pythons are sometimes placed in a family of their own, the Pythonidae, all of which are oviparous. Boas, on the other hand, are live-bearers, and most species occur in the New World, a few species also on Madagascar and in the South-west Pacific: the sand boas widespread from eastern Africa to India, and also in southern Europe. Pythons are widespread in Africa, Australasia and Asia. The world's largest snakes, living and fossil, belong to this family, that includes the Anaconda and the Reticulated Python, both reportedly reaching 10m.

## Common Sand Boa *Eryx conicus* 1.00m

A stout, keeled, medium-sized snake from arid and semi-arid regions. Head scarcely distinct from neck; body short, cylindrical; mental groove absent; snout rounded; nostrils and eyes small, the latter with vertical pupils; a pair of spurs on each side of vent; tail short, tapering to an acute point; tail scales strong keeled; dorsum brownish grey, with a series of large, irregular dark brown or reddish-brown blotches, sometimes joined or forming a zig zag band. Abundant at some arid localities, such as sandy beaches or in loose soil. Mostly active at dusk and at night, when they emerge from rodent burrows to forage on small mammals and birds, which are typically caught in ambush and killed by constriction. Mating takes place in November. Ovoviviparous, a litter of 3–16 is produced. Widely distributed in the drier parts of western and Peninsular India, Pakistan, Nepal, Sri Lanka, with an unconfirmed record from Bangladesh. A large number of these snakes are caught every year for the leather industry. These snakes can be aggressive, and bites are painful. Nevertheless, both this and the Red Sand Boa are displayed by snake-charmers.

## Red Sand Boa *Eryx johnii* 1.25m

A stout, smooth snake from arid regions. Head indistinct from neck; chin with a mental groove; eyes small with vertical pupils; spur present on each side of vent; tail short, blunt, superficially similar in form to head; dorsum of adults grey, brownish red or dark brown, uniformly coloured or with indistinct black spots; belly paler; juveniles paler, with a series of dark spots or cross-bars. Found in loose soil, and prefers semi-deserts and coastal scrub. Crepuscular and nocturnal, ambushing small mammals and birds. Mating takes place between April and May, and after a gestation period of 4 months, litters of 6–8 young are produced. This is a 'twin-headed' snake, commonly exhibited by itinerant snake charmers. Distributed over western and Peninsular India, Pakistan, Afghanistan, Iran and Nepal.

## Whitaker's Sand Boa *Eryx whitakeri* 79cm

A medium-sized sand boa, restricted to the moist west coast of India, and named for the Indian herpetologist, Romulus Whitaker. Head small, distinct from the cylindrical body; forehead scales small, smooth; mental groove absent; males with a claw-like spur on each side of vent; tail short, slightly prehensile, with a blunt tip, especially in adults; dorsum brownish grey or dark brown, with even darker blotches that are joined and extend up to the middle half of body, forming a band with irregular edges; belly unpatterned grey. Inhabits scrub forests and sea beaches, and is fossorial. Diet comprises small mice. Distributed in Kerala, Karnataka, Goa and Maharashtra.

## Indian Rock Python *Python molurus* 7.62m

A constricting snake, large individuals of which could be dangerous to humans. Head lance-shaped; sensory pits in rostral, first two supralabials and some infralabials; mental groove present; tail short, prehensile; dorsum yellowish grey to dark brown above, with a series of 30–40 large, squarish dark grey or brown marks; flanks with blotches. Inhabits forests and scrubland, in burrows of porcupines, bears and rodents. Diet includes rodents, monitor lizards and deer. Mates December–February and clutch size is 8–107, eggs 120 × 60mm, deposited in damp soil and guarded by female. Incubation period 58–72 days. Known from India, as well as Pakistan, Nepal, Sri Lanka, Bangladesh, east to the Malay Peninsula and western Indonesia.

## Reticulated Python *Python reticulatus* 9.80m

Largest and heaviest Indian snake. Yellow or light brown above, with a series of dark brown spots, each edged with black; a black streak along forehead and another on each side of head, from eye to angle of jaws. Forages after dark on edges of rivers, in primary forests, as well as in and around human settlements. Diet includes birds and mammals as large as deer. Clutch size 15–100; eggs taking 65–105 days to hatch. Hatchlings 60–75cm. Occurs in the extreme north-eastern state of Arunachal Pradesh and on Nicobar Islands, within Indian limits, and south-east Asia.

15

# COLUBRIDAE ('TYPICAL SNAKES')

The so-called 'typical snakes' include a huge assemblage (worldwide with nearly 2,000 species) of snakes, that vary in their mode of life, from burrowing forms, to terrestrial ones and arboreal and aquatic types. There is, thus, nothing typical about this group, and the name derives from the fact that most of the common (and once best known) snakes of Europe belong to this family. Although a majority of these species are harmless, a few have proven to have lethal bites, such as some of keelback snakes; while others, with their enlarged teeth, such as cat snakes and kukri snakes, need to be handled with care.

**Common Vine Snake** *Ahaetulla nasuta* 2.00m

A bright green, long and slender snake, with a very long snout that ends in a pointed tip; having a groove in front of the large eyes; pupils forming horizontal slits; dorsally bright green, although it may also be olive-brown, with a longitudinal, yellowish line along the outer margin of the ventrals. Abundant in lightly forested habitats, including gardens, frequenting trees and bushes, from the plains to hills up to 1,800m. Diurnal, it waits in ambush for lizards, birds and small mammals. Tadpoles have also been recorded in the diet of this species. It bites readily, the enlarged rear fang causing mild pain that may produce itchiness and slight swelling locally. Ovoviviparous, mating known in June. Between 3–23 young are born between March and December, after 172 days; these measure 35cm in length. Inhabits peninsular India, in addition to Bangladesh, Nepal, Sri Lanka, and the northern part of mainland south-east Asia, including Myanmar and Thailand. In many parts of the range of this and related species, they are referred to as 'eye-pluckers', which is also the source of the generic name (from the Sinhala language of Sri Lanka).

## Oriental Vine Snake *Ahaetulla prasina* 1.85m

A long-nosed, bright green tree snake, although its snout is not as long as that of the Common Vine Snake. Snout elongated; tail comprising one-third of body length; eye with a horizontal pupil and a groove along the snout, before the eyes. The coloration of this usually green snake can also be brown and there is a yellow stripe along each side of the body; the belly light green. A forest-dwelling snake, found on low vegetation, such as shrubs and saplings, it also comes into parks and gardens in search of lizards and birds. Usually aggressive and quick to bite, it has a mildly toxic saliva. A threat display comprises expanding its neck to reveal the black and white skin between the scales. Curious among snakes is the habit of these snakes to stick their tongue out of their mouth for a long time. Ovoviviparous, it produces 4–6 live young that are light brown in colour. Distributed in north-eastern India, and the range includes south-east Asia.

## Beddome's Keelback *Amphiesma beddomei* 69cm

A forest-dwelling species, commonly encountered along forest streams, as well as away from them. Body relatively slender; scales keeled; dorsum olive-brown, with a series of yellow spots, enclosed by two black spots or short bars; oblique, black-edged, yellow stripe from eye to angle of jaws; lips yellow; belly cream, unpatterned or dotted with brown on the sides. Juveniles have a yellow collar. Found in evergreen and moist deciduous forests, in the mid-hills. Diurnal and crepuscular, active on edges of water bodies, such as stream banks. These snakes are predators of toads and frogs. Widespread in the hills of Maharashtra, Karnataka, Kerala and western Tamil Nadu States in western India.

# Günther's Keelback *Amphiesma khasiense* 60cm

A montane species of keelback from north-eastern India. Small to medium-sized snake; scales keeled; dorsum brown with small regularly arranged black spots; lips cream with dark margins or entirely dark; a series of yellow spots on the sides that may be joined; belly yellow, with black spots that are sometimes joined. Known from forests at elevations of 600–1,500m. Nothing is known of its diet or reproduction. Besides Meghalaya State, this snake has been recorded from Myanmar, Thailand, Laos and Vietnam.

## Eastern Keelback *Amphiesma platyceps* 88cm

A small to medium-sized, slender snake; dorsum dark grey, bronze-brown, reddish brown or yellowish brown; sometimes with a dark lateral stripe; a dark band from rostral through eye to last supralabial; a nuchal loop sometimes present; belly yellowish cream or with an orange tinge, sometimes with small dark streaks, especially posteriorly; throat often powdered with black. Inhabits forest edges as well as unlogged forests, and also agricultural fields and in the proximity of human dwellings. Crepuscular, its diet comprises skinks, frogs and small lizards. Two eggs, 8 × 25mm, are produced. Distributed in the foothills and middle elevations of the Himalayas of India and Nepal.

## Buff-striped Keelback *Amphiesma stolatum* 80cm

A dainty striped snake from the lowlands. Two bright longitudinal stripes along olive-grey to greenish-grey dorsum; buff or orange stripes dorso-laterally. Inhabits grasslands, as well as lowland forests, usually in the vicinity of lakes and ponds, as well as rice fields. Active in the mornings and at dusk, when they hunt frogs, insects, scorpions, fish and lizards. Clutches of 3–15 eggs, measuring 22–35 × 13–18mm, hatch 36–62 days later; two clutches may be produced in a year. Widespread in India, in addition to Pakistan, Nepal, Sri Lanka, Bangladesh, and south-east Asia.

## Venning's Keelback *Amphiesma venningi* 68cm

A little-known keelback from north-eastern India. Body relatively slender; scales feebly keeled, outer scale rows smooth; dorsum greyish brown, with indistinct black squares; sometimes an incomplete collar; juveniles with yellow chain-like markings on the sides; belly coral red or bright orange, edged with dark brown. Inhabits forested habitats in the midhills. Diet comprises tadpoles. Known from Myanmar, southern China, and Meghalaya and Arunachal Pradesh.

## Banded Racer *Argyrogena fasciolatus* 1.40m

A slender and swift snake. Snout strongly projecting; dorsal scales smooth; adults brown, sometimes with a brick-red tint, anteriorly with narrow white, brown and black cross-bars; posterior, with indistinct dark cross-bars or spots; belly unpatterned yellow or cream. Juveniles with white pattern on a dark dorsum, with narrow cross-bars on anterior of body. Inhabits forests in the plains, in dense bushes, parks and gardens, concealing itself in rat holes and under rock piles. Diurnal and terrestrial, its diet comprises rodents, shrews, bats, frogs and lizards. Clutches of 2–7 eggs, laid in January, hatch in July. Known from the Indian Peninsula, besides Bangladesh and Nepal.

## Olive Keelback Water Snake *Atretium schistosum* 1.00m

A small to medium-sized snake from moist areas close to water bodies. Snout short; nostrils slit-like, placed on top of snout; scales distinctly keeled, lacking apical pits; dorsum olive-brown or greenish grey, unpatterned or with two series of small black spots, occasionally a dark lateral streak; upper lip, outer row of scales and belly yellow. Fond of damp places near water on the plains, and is also known from brackish coastal areas and near agricultural fields. Diurnal, it is found near water bodies and other moist areas, and is a good swimmer as well as being adept in climbing low bushes. Diet comprises frogs, tadpoles, fish, prawns and crabs. Clutches of 10–32 eggs are laid between December to April, eggs 25–35mm and hatchlings 16.5–17.5cm. Known from the Indian Peninsula, in addition to Nepal, Bangladesh and Sri Lanka.

## Iridescent Snake *Blythia reticulata* 41cm

Ashok Sohrab Captain/The Lisus

A small, little-known, forest-dwelling species. Head scarcely distinct from body; scales smooth, without apical pits; tail short; dorsum olive to dark, highly iridescent; scales sometimes light specked or bordered; juveniles with a cream border, with a gap on the vertebral line. Inhabits evergreen forests at medium altitudes and is semi-fossorial. Little is known of its natural history, except that it is oviparous. Indian records are from Assam, Arunachal Pradesh and Manipur States, and the species also occurs in Myanmar.

## Andamans Cat Snake *Boiga andamanensis* 1.30m

A little-known, arboreal, lizard-eating snake from the Andaman Islands. Head distinct from neck; vertebral scales strongly enlarged; the several closely related species of cat snake from India differentiable only in scale counts; this species shows mid-dorsal scale rows 21 and subcaudal scales numbers 118–133; dorsum greyish brown with a series of dark brown vertebral spots; belly yellowish cream. Found in forested areas as well as in human habitation, such as the thatched roofs of houses. Forages at night. Diet comprises lizards; breeding habits unknown. A rear-fanged snake, not of medical importance because of its small size. Restricted to the Andaman Islands in the Bay of Bengal.

## Sri Lankan Cat Snake *Boiga ceylonensis* 1.32m

Another tree-living, lizard-eating snake from the Western Ghats. Head distinct from neck; vertebral scales strongly enlarged; the several closely related species of cat snake found in India are differentiable only in scale counts; this species shows mid-dorsal scale rows 19 and subcaudal scales numbers 98–108; dorsum light tan; a transverse bar on neck meeting a long streak on the nape; a series of alternating dark brown and pale chevrons; belly cream flecked with brown. Inhabits evergreen forests, where they are found on shrubs as well as on the ground. Hides in hollow tree trunks and in the grass during the day, venturing out at night to hunt. When threatened, it raises its body into loops, vibrating the tail-tip and attempts to bite. It is mildly venomous and equipped with rear-fangs but, because of its small size, is not of medical importance. Diet comprises geckos and agamid lizards. Males are much larger than females. Oviparous, 3–10 eggs, measuring 25–29 × 8–13mm are laid between February and April; hatchlings measure 29–33cm in length. Besides the Western Ghats of Peninsular India, this species is known from Sri Lanka.

## Travancore Cat Snake *Boiga dightoni* 1.10m

A little-known tree snake from the Western Ghats. Head distinct from neck; vertebral scales enlarged; dorsum reddish brown or pale brown, with darker blotches on the back; head with small dark dots; belly yellow or yellowish brown, finely dotted with brown. Inhabits forested habitats in the mid-hills, including secondary forests, and shrubs. Nocturnal in activity. Lizards, such as the Garden Lizard, are known to be eaten by this arboreal species. A rear-fanged snake, not of medical importance because of its small size. Restricted to Travancore and Ponmudi Hills of Kerala State and Anaimalai and Palni Hills of western Tamil Nadu.

## Forsten's Cat Snake *Boiga forsteni* 2.30m

A slender, highly arboreal snake. Head triangular; vertebral scale row is enlarged; dorsum greyish brown, with a series of large distinct brown cross-bars anteriorly; scales smooth, with apical pits; belly unpatterned cream or spotted with brown. Inhabits forested tracks and agricultural fields in the lowlands and is arboreal. At night, it emerges to feed on lizards, birds, bats, rodents and other snakes. Oviparous, laying 5–10 eggs between August and September. A bite from this snake should be taken seriously. Widespread from the foothills of the Himalayas to Peninsular India. Also Nepal and Sri Lanka.

## Many-banded Cat Snake *Boiga multifasciata* 88cm

Frank Tillack

A slender, brown cat snake. Head distinct from neck, triangular; scales smooth with apical pits; vertebral scales slightly enlarged; dorsum greyish brown, speckled with black, narrow black, transverse or oblique bars that sometimes form V-shaped marks, with a white spot in the middle; a black longitudinal stripe on nape and two more on forehead; belly cream, speckled with black. Inhabits forested areas, and is arboreal and nocturnal in habit, feeding on birds, small mammals and lizards. Oviparous. Distributed along the Himalayan foothills, from Himachal Pradesh to eastern India (northern West Bengal and Sikkim), in addition to Nepal.

## Many-spotted Cat Snake *Boiga multomaculata* 99cm

A small, lizard-eating cat snake with a relatively more triangular head than its relatives. Body laterally compressed, slender; scales smooth; dorsum grey-brown, with a black line from the back of the eye to the jaws; 2 brown lines, edged with black from snout to back of head; a series of irregular marks of the same colour over the body, the ones on the top larger than those on the sides; belly greyish brown, with small brown spots. A species from lowland and submontane forests, it is arboreal, inhabiting short trees, bushes and bamboo groves. It is a rather non-aggressive snake that feeds primarily on lizards, sometimes entering houses in search of geckos. Clutches of 5–7 take 60 days to hatch. A rear-fanged snake, not of medical importance because of its small size. Known from north-eastern India, besides Bangladesh, and also from eastern China and mainland south-east Asia.

## Collared Cat Snake *Boiga nuchalis* 1.32m

A cat snake with a collar-like marking. Head distinct from neck; eyes large, with vertical pupils; scales smooth, with apical pits; vertebral scales enlarged; dorsum light purplish brown to pale greyish brown, with a vertebral series of dark transverse spots; an oblique narrow black streak from eye to angle of mouth; belly yellow, densely speckled with purplish brown. Inhabits forested areas; nocturnal and arboreal, feeding on frogs, lizards, snakes, birds and small mammals. Oviparous. Known from Himalayan foothills to Assam and the Western Ghats, besides Nepal.

# Tawny Cat Snake *Boiga ochracea* 1.10m

*Subspecies* stoliczkae

A cat snake from the eastern part of the country. Head distinct from neck; scales smooth, with apical pits; vertebral scale row greatly enlarged; dorsum reddish brown, ochre or coral red; unpatterned or with a poorly-defined dark transverse line; a dark streak from eye to angle of mouth. Inhabits forests, parks and gardens. Arboreal, and nocturnal and/or crepuscular. Diet comprises birds and their eggs, small mammals and lizards. Oviparous. Known from eastern and north-eastern India, in addition to Nepal, Myanmar and Thailand.

# Common Indian Cat Snake *Boiga trigonata* 1.25m

A long, thin, snake found on thatched roofs of village houses. Head distinct from neck; eyes large; scales smooth, with apical pits; vertebral scales feebly enlarged; dorsum yellow to greyish brown, with a series of light grey, arrow-head shaped markings; a narrow dark streak, bordered above with light grey runs from behind eye to angle of mouth; belly white or grey, speckled with dark grey spots. Inhabits forested areas, as well as parks and gardens. Nocturnal and arboreal, feeding on lizards and birds, their eggs and small mammals. Clutches of 3–11 are produced between August and October, eggs 10–15 × 30–39mm. Incubation is 35–43 days and hatchlings are 23.7–26.5cm. Widespread in the Indian Peninsula, it ranges from the Middle East, up to Pakistan, India, Sri Lanka and Nepal.

25

**Nicobarese Cat Snake** *Boiga wallachi* 1.05m

A large, bright yellow species of cat snake, from the Nicobar Islands. Head small, distinct from neck; snout long, greater than eye and projecting beyond lower jaw; eye large, with vertically elliptical pupil; dorsal scales smooth, lacking apical pits; dorsum yellowish brown, each scale with a brownish-olive tinge; lips unpatterned yellow; no dark stripe behind eye; belly bright yellow, with dark rounded blotches on abdomen and under tail. Nocturnal and terrestrial, inhabiting lowland rainforests. Bird eggs have been recorded in the diet of this species. A rear-fanged snake, not of medical importance because of its small size. Restricted to the island of Great Nicobar in the Bay of Bengal.

**Yellow-banded Mangrove Snake** *Cantoria violacea* 1.20m

A slender water snake from the Andaman Islands. Body relatively long, slender and cylindrical; head scarcely distinct from neck; dorsal and ventral scales smooth and tail slightly compressed; dorsum dark blackish grey or black with yellow transverse bars that are narrower than the interspace areas; head white-spotted; belly cream or with grey markings. Inhabits coastal rivers, including estuaries and presumably feeds on fish. Nothing is known of its reproductive biology. Besides the Andaman Islands, it is known from the south-east Asian mainland and islands.

**Dog-faced Water Snake** *Cerberus rynchops* 1.25m

A common water snake from mangrove swamps and river mouths, with a projecting upper-jaw, giving it a dog-like appearance. Head long and distinct from neck; eyes beady, with rounded pupil; scales distinctly keeled; dorsum dark grey, with faint dark blotches and a dark line across eyes; belly yellowish cream, with dark grey areas. Abundant in mangrove mudflats and rice fields, where they hide in crab holes, emerging at night. Diet comprises fish, such as mudskippers and gobies, as well as crabs and frogs. Between 6–30 young are born, remaining together for a while before dispersing. Widespread along the east coast of India, the Andaman and Nicobar Islands, the range of the species extends to Australia.

**Ornate Flying Snake** *Chrysopelea ornata* 1.75m

This snake is capable of spectacular glides of at least 50m between trees, when body is flattened like a ribbon. Medium-sized, slender, with depressed head; ventrals with pronounced keels laterally; vertebral scales not enlarged; dorsal scales smooth or feebly keeled, with apical pits; dorsum greenish yellow or pale green; orange or red spots between dark cross-bands; head black dorsally, with yellow and black cross-bars; belly pale green with series of black lateral spots. Inhabits old growth trees, secondary vegetation, cultivations and enters houses. Diurnal, arboreal. Feeds on lizards, also bats, rodents, birds and small snakes. Oviparous, 6–20 eggs between May and June. Eggs 13–18 × 26–38mm, incubation 65–80 days. Hatchlings 15–26cm. In India range includes foothills of Himalayas, to Uttar Pradesh, northeastern India and southern Gujarat, south to the Western Ghats.

## Yellow-striped Trinket Snake *Coelognathus flavolineatus* 1.80m

A fast-moving, rat-eating snake, widespread in south-east Asia. Body rather slender; scales keeled; tail about a quarter the snout–vent length; dorsum brownish grey, with a dark stripe from behind eye to above back of mouth, and another one along nape; several short dark stripes or elongated blotches present on top and sides of body. Terrestrial and arboreal, inhabiting forested areas in the lowlands, as well as in more disturbed habitats, such as parks and gardens. When cornered, it rears up, raising a third of the body, with the neck coiled into a curve. Diet includes rodents and birds, as well as frogs and lizards. Large prey is usually restrained in a coil and constricted. Clutches include 5–12 eggs, which take 75–90 days to hatch. Besides the Andamans, it is known from mainland south-east Asia, in addition to Java, Borneo and Sumatra.

## Copper-headed Trinket Snake *Coelognathus radiatus* 2.30m

Another rat-eating snake, this one is more common in open areas, such as grasslands, ascending the hills up to 1,400m. Body rather slender; snout relatively long; scales keeled; dorsum greyish brown or yellowish brown, with four black stripes along the front of the body; a cream stripe runs along the upper two wide stripes; the lower stripes are narrower and generally broken up; head copper-brown, with 3 black radiating lines from the eyes. When threatened, it too rears its head and part of its body, throwing the neck and body into a coil in a position to attack. Active during the cool hours of the morning, and again at dusk. Its diet comprises birds and rats. Between 5–12 eggs are produced at a time and hatch after 70–95 days; up to 4 clutches may be produced in a year. Widespread in the Indian region, the range of the species extends into southern China, mainland south-east Asia, Java, Borneo and Sumatra.

## Indian Smooth Snake *Coronella brachyura* 52cm

A rare, little known, cylindrical snake from the dry western Indian Peninsula. Head scarcely distinct from neck; eye relatively large, with rounded pupil; nostril large; scales smooth, with apical pits; dorsum olive-brown, with faint light variegations on the head and front part of body; belly unpatterned cream. Nothing is known of its diet or reproductive habits. Known from isolated localities in the plains of western peninsular India, including Maharashtra State.

## Blue Bronzeback Tree Snake *Dendrelaphis cyanochloris* 1.33m

A beautiful tree snake from the Andaman Islands and also eastern India. Head distinct from body, slightly flattened, scales smooth; dorsum olive, scales edged with black, a broad black stripe from the head to beyond the neck, breaking up into spots; belly yellow. When threatened, it expands its neck, revealing the blue skin under the scales, and the resulting effect is a blue with brown barred neck and body. It is diurnal, and known from both primary forests and cultivated areas. Diet comprises lizards and possibly also frogs. Nothing is known of its breeding biology. Known from northern West Bengal and Assam, the islands of the Andamans group, in addition to Myanmar, Laos and Thailand.

**Large-eyed Bronzeback Tree Snake** *Dendrelaphis grandoculis* 1.28m

A little-known tree snake from the Western Ghats. Snout relatively broad and somewhat square; eyes large; dorsum olive-brown, with scattered small black blotches; eyes bordered with white; dark lateral stripes along eyes and body absent; belly olive, darkening posteriorly; tail with a black line on each side, and one on the lower surface. A diurnal, arboreal species, active in trees and shrubs. Diet and reproductive habits are unknown. Restricted to Travancore, Silent Valley, Tirunelveli and Nilgiri Hills of Kerala and western Tamil Nadu States.

**Painted Bronzeback Tree Snake** *Dendrelaphis pictus* 1.25m

(Top) *Subspecies* pictus; (above) *subspecies* andamanensis

An elegant, slender tree snake that can make spectacular leaps between treetops. Head distinct from neck; eyes large with rounded pupils; iris golden; tail nearly one-third total length; dorsal scales smooth and narrow except for two outer rows, with apical pits; dorsum bronze-brown or brownish olive, with a yellow or cream stripe, edged with black along flanks; forehead brown with a black lateral stripe from nasal opening to neck; blue or greenish-blue skin patch on neck that is displayed when excited. Inhabits forested areas, but will also come into plantations and around human habitation. When molested, it exudes a foul-smelling musk from its anal glands. Diurnal and arboreal, it hunts frogs and lizards. Clutches comprise 3–8 eggs, measuring 9–11 × 22–39mm, and several clutches may be produced a year. Incubation period is 75–76 days and hatchlings measure 20–30cm. Distributed in eastern and north-eastern India (subspecies *pictus*) and the Nicobar Islands (subspecies *andamanensis*): also, Bangladesh, Nepal, and eastwards to south-east Asia.

# Common Bronzeback Tree Snake *Dendrelaphis tristis* 1.50m

A long, graceful tree snake. Eyes large, lustrous, with rounded pupils and golden iris; tail about a third total length; scales smooth; dorsum unpatterned purplish- or bronzy-brown, vertebral scales on neck and forebody yellow; with a buff flank stripe from neck to vent; light blue on neck between scales that is revealed during a display; belly pale grey, green or yellow. Inhabits open areas, such as disturbed forests, forest clearings and around human habitation in rural areas, especially on thatched roofs of houses. Diurnal and arboreal, but also known to forage on land and at the edge of water. They can make long jumps between trees. Diet comprises frogs and lizards, and also bird eggs and insects. Oviparous, probably breeding continuously; clutches of 6–7 are deposited in tree hollows or deserted bird nests; eggs 10–12 × 29–39mm and incubation period 4–6 weeks, eggs hatching in June. Distributed throughout India, in addition to Pakistan, Sri Lanka and Nepal.

# Eastern Trinket Snake *Othriophis cantoris* 1.96m

Frank Tillack

A mountain-dwelling snake from the middle elevations of the Eastern Himalayas and north-eastern India. A large-growing species; head slightly distinct from neck; ventral keel distinct, dorsum greyish brown to yellowish brown, the dark or light scale borders producing a reticulate pattern, on top of which are dark brown or reddish-brown blotches that form transverse bands towards the end of the body; belly yellow, becoming pink towards the tail. A montane species, distributed at altitudes of 1,000–2,300m, where it inhabits forested habitats. Diet remains unknown, and is likely to be small mammals, such as rats, and also birds. Clutches of 10 are produced towards the end of July. Apart from northern West Bengal, Sikkim and Meghalaya States, it is known from Nepal and northern Myanmar.

## Khasi Hills Trinket Snake *Elaphe frenata* 1.50m

A medium- to large-sized, rat-eating, green snake from north-eastern India. Snout rather long; body is distinctly compressed; ventral keels developed; long, prehensile tail; dorsum grass-green to olive; lips light green; a black stripe from behind the eyes to the angle of jaws; belly pale green to white. Arboreal, inhabiting shrubs and low trees in evergreen forests. Lizards, rats and birds comprise the diet of this snake. Nothing is known of its breeding habits. Indian records are from Meghalaya and Arunachal Pradesh. Also known from Vietnam and eastern China.

## Indian Trinket Snake *Coelognathus helena* 1.68m

*Subspecies* helena

*Subspecies* monticollaris

Another rat-eating snake, this one is a widespread forest-dwelling snake. A medium-sized, relatively slender snake, scales smooth on the sides, weakly keeled posteriorly; dorsum brown or olive, with transverse bands and/or with blotches on the sides; neck with two dark narrow lines or a dark-edged, white collar. Found in the plains and the hills up to an elevation of 900m, from forests and plantations, especially in the vicinity of water bodies. When threatened, it rears its head and part of its body, throwing the neck and body into a coil in a position to attack. Terrestrial, although capable of climbing and crepuscular in habit. Its diet comprises rats, lizards and birds. Between 3–12 eggs are produced at a time, and more than a single clutch may be laid in a year. Widespread in the Indian region, the subspecies *helena* from the plains, *monticollaris* from the Western Ghats.

## Himalayan Trinket Snake *Orthriophis hodgsonii* 2.10m

A high altitude, rat-eating snake from the Himalayas. A slender species; ventral keels developed; dorsum olive-brown, some scales bordered with black and white, resulting in a reticulate pattern; head, including lips, yellow; a large dark blotch in centre of forehead; belly yellow with dark spots. Found at altitudes of 1,000–3,200m above sea level, from moist deciduous forests, as well as oak forests, in addition to edges of agricultural fields in the vicinity of water. Diet includes toads and skinks. Oviparous. Himalayas, from Kashmir to Meghalaya States, besides Nepal and Tibet.

## Green Trinket Snake *Elaphe prasina* 1.20m

A green species of tree snake, which is seldom seen and consequently, its habits are little known. Body relatively slender; snout long; head slightly distinct from neck; ventral keels well developed; tail rather long; dorsum uniformly green, sometimes with a brown tail tip; lips and belly pale green; a faint dark stripe behind the eyes. Inhabits forested hills, at elevations of 850–2,560m, although lowland localities are also known. Diurnal and arboreal, it is known from bamboo clumps, as well as from the roofs of thatched houses. Diet includes reptiles, such as lizards, and also small mammals and birds. Between 5–8 eggs are produced in March–May, and hatch after 58–60 days; hatchlings measure 23cm in total length. Besides northern West Bengal, Assam, Meghalaya, Manipur, Arunachal Pradesh, this species is known from Myanmar, China, Vietnam, Thailand and Peninsular Malaysia.

**Common Smooth Water Snake** *Enhydris enhydris* 81cm

A common water snake from southern and south-eastern Asia. Head rather small, body medium-sized, stout and cylindrical; head somewhat depressed and only slightly distinct from neck; snout rounded; nostrils situated on upper surface of head; pupils vertical; dorsal scales smooth, lacking apical pits; dorsum greyish brown or olive-green, typically with a dark vertebral and two light lateral stripes from upper surface of head to tail; belly yellowish cream, with a dark line along each side. Inhabits freshwater, and sometimes also brackish water, including slow-moving rivers, marshes, lakes and wet rice fields. Diet comprises fish, frogs, tadpoles and, sometimes, lizards. Mating occurs in October, and this snake is ovoviviparous, producing several clutches a year, between January and June, each comprising 4–20 young that measure 15.5cm. Widespread in eastern India, besides Nepal, Bangladesh, east to southern China and south-east Asia.

**White-bellied Mangrove Snake** *Fordonia leucobalia* 95cm

Mark O'Shea

An extremely variable water snake in terms of coloration, found in mangrove areas and other portions of the river close to the sea. Head short, wide, scarcely wider than neck; head scales large and distinct; loreal absent; lower jaw short and scales smooth. Variable in coloration and pattern, this snake may be dark grey or brown, with light spots, or light grey, yellow or orange with dark spots; belly pale cream, sometimes with small, dark spots; lips yellowish cream. Inhabits tidal rivers. Crabs form the main component of the diet of this snake, although small fish are also consumed. Ovoviviparous, producing 10–15 young at a time, hatchlings measuring 18cm. This coastal species is known from the Andaman Islands, within India, its range extending through the south-east Asian mainland and islands to New Guinea and northern Australia.

**Glossy Marsh Snake** *Gerarda prevostiana* 53cm

Another little-known snake from mangrove swamps. Head distinct from neck; eye small with vertically elliptical pupil; body relatively long; scales smooth; tail short; dorsum unpatterned grey or brown; lips and lower scales of dorsum cream; belly brownish cream, with median dark streaks. Inhabits coastal areas, including mangrove swamps and is nocturnal. Soft-shelled crabs form the mainstay of the diet of this species, although fish and shrimps are also eaten. Occurs on both coasts of India, besides Sri Lanka, as well as isolated localities in south-east Asia, including Myanmar, Thailand and the Malay Peninsula.

**Red-tailed Trinket Snake** *Gonyosoma oxycephalum* 2.40m

A beautiful, green snake, with a russet or red tail. A rather thick-set snake, at least when fully grown, with an elongated, coffin-shaped head that is slightly wider than the neck; scales feebly keeled or smooth. The body of adults is emerald green, with a light green throat and a black stripe along the sides of the head, across the eyes; belly yellow; juveniles are olive-brown with narrow, white bars towards the back of the body. It is arboreal and perhaps also quite terrestrial, evidenced by the numbers found killed on roads. Diet includes rodents, such as rats and squirrels, as well as birds. Several clutches are produced annually, eggs numbering 5–12, 65mm in length, and take approximately 100–120 days to hatch. Recorded from the Andaman Islands, besides being widespread in mainland and insular regions of south-east Asia.

## Stripe-necked Snake *Liopeltis frenatus* 76cm

A small and slender snake with a cylindrical body and a relatively long tail. Head not depressed; snout not projecting; scales smooth, lacking apical pits; dorsum olive, scales edged with black, sometimes also with white, forming longitudinal stripes on the front half of the body; a broad black stripe from the back of the eye on to neck; upper lip and belly cream. Inhabits subtropical and montane forests at altitudes of 600–1,800m. Terrestrial, the diet and reproductive habits of this species remain unknown. Indian records are from north-east, including Meghalaya and Assam States; the species is also recorded from northern Myanmar, Laos and Vietnam.

## Common Wolf Snake *Lycodon aulicus* 80cm

A common, house-dwelling species. Head flattened; snout projecting beyond lower jaw; scales smooth; dorsum brown or greyish brown, with 12–19 white cross-bars, sometimes speckled with brown, that expand laterally, enclosing triangular patches; belly cream or yellowish white. Inhabits lowlands, in parks and human habitation, where they occupy thatched roofs. Nocturnal, emerging after dark to feed on geckos, snakes and rodents. Oviparous, producing 3–11 eggs between February and July, 25–32mm, and more than 1 clutch may be produced a year. Hatchlings emerge in September and October, and measure 14–19cm. Distributed all over India, in addition to Bangladesh, Nepal, Sri Lanka and Myanmar.

## Island Wolf Snake *Lycodon capucinus* 70cm

A familiar south-east Asian house snake, occurring within Indian limits only in the Andaman Islands. Head flattened; snout rounded; scales smooth; a brown or purple snake, usually with a narrow yellow or cream band at the back of the head that may be spotted with brown; scales of body light-edged to form indistinct crossbars; belly cream or light yellow. It inhabits forested tracts, and is nocturnal, emerging at dusk to catch lizards, such as geckos and skinks, that may be caught in its coils and constricted. Occasionally enters houses, presumably in search of geckos. Clutches include 3–11 eggs, incubation period being 45 days, while the female remains near the eggs. The species is widespread in southeast Asia, both on the mainland and on the islands.

## Yellow-spotted Wolf Snake *Lycodon flavomaculatus* 35cm

A yellow-spotted, dark wolf snake from the foothills of the Western Ghats. Snout obtusely rounded, somewhat flattened; head weakly differentiated from neck; dorsum black, with a series of small yellow spots, adjacent to which bars of same colour descend and broaden to form reticulation on sides, giving it a barred appearance; supralabials nine and only the first supralabial contacts nasal. Of its diet and reproductive habits, nothing is on record. Known from isolated localities in Maharashtra State, in western Peninsular India.

## Yellow-speckled Wolf Snake *Lycodon jara* 55cm

A finely-spotted species of wolf snake from north-eastern India. A small snake, with a fairly long head; snout somewhat flattened, not projecting beyond lower jaw; ventrals not angular laterally; dorsum brown or purplish black, finely stippled throughout with paired yellowish-white spots or short longitudinal lines on each scale; upper lip and lower surface unpatterned white; a white collar in juveniles. Inhabits both forests and open areas with bushes and scattered trees and agricultural areas. Diet comprises frogs, lizards and small mammals. Oviparous. Known from north-eastern India and Nepal.

## Barred Wolf Snake *Lycodon striatus* 43cm

A small, ground-dwelling snake. Snout flattened; head weakly differentiated from neck; supralabials eight, first and second of which contact nasal; dorsum black to dark brown, with a series of white or yellow transverse marks, distance between which diminishes towards tail; upper lips and belly unpatterned white. Inhabits dry regions, including forest edges and semi-deserts, hiding under stones during the day and emerging at night to forage. Diet comprises lizards, such as geckos and skinks. Clutches are 2–4, eggs relatively large at 9–12 × 25–30mm and laid in April. Parental care of eggs known. Widespread from central Asia to India, including Pakistan, Sri Lanka and Nepal.

## Travancore Wolf Snake *Lycodon travancoricus* 63cm

*Howard Bradley Shaffer*

A widespread species of wolf snake from the low hills and plains of the Indian Peninsula. Snout broad, slightly depressed; scales smooth; dorsum dark purplish brown or nearly black, bearing pale yellow cross-bars that bifurcate on the sides, enclosing triangular spots; all bars speckled with black; upper lip typically brown, spotted with white; belly unpatterned cream. Inhabits deciduous and evergreen forests and is nocturnal. Nothing is known of its diet or natural history. Known from isolated localities in the states of Maharashtra, Kerala, Tamil Nadu, Madhya Pradesh, Orissa and Andhra Pradesh.

## White-barred Kukri Snake *Oligodon albocinctus* 76cm

A small to medium-sized, brownish-red snake from eastern India. Body cylindrical; the head is short, snout-tip blunt and rounded; eye with rounded pupil; scales smooth, lacking any apical pits; dorsum brownish red, sometimes with white, yellow or fawn-coloured, black-edged cross-bars, numbering 19–27 on body and 4–8 on tail, or with dark brown, black-edged spots; forehead with a dark stripe from the upper lips to the eyes, a dark V-shaped stripe from angle of mouth across parietals, sometimes interrupted and a dark broad V-shaped marking on back of head; belly cream, yellow or coral-red, marked with black. Inhabits forested habitats, and is sometimes found in tea gardens. Terrestrial, with a crepuscular activity cycle. Diet comprises rodents, frogs, lizards and their eggs, juveniles taking insects. Oviparous. Known from eastern India (Sikkim and northern West Bengal) as well as north-eastern India. Also, Bhutan, Nepal, east to Myanmar.

*Ashok Sohrab Captain/The Lisus*

## Banded Kukri Snake *Oligodon arnensis* 64cm

Superficially resembles the venomous banded krait, although this is a completely harmless snake. A small snake; body stout and cylindrical; snout short and blunt; scales smooth; dorsum brown, usually with red or purple markings, lighter on flanks, with 32–41 black cross-bars or transversely arranged spots that break up on flanks into streaks, sometimes edged with cream; bars 1–5 scales wide; head with three dark, arrowhead-shaped marks; belly cream with indistinct lateral spots. Inhabits forests, as well as disturbed habitats, such as parks and gardens, and may enter houses. A ground-dwelling species, it inhabits the leaf litter of the forest floor, and also the crevices of rocks and tree holes. Both diurnal and nocturnal, although most activities are during the day or on cool rainy nights. Diet comprises small rodents, lizards and reptile eggs. Elongate eggs, numbering 4–9, measuring 36 × 10mm, are produced. Widespread in Peninsular India, besides Pakistan, Nepal and Sri Lanka.

## Spot-tailed Kukri Snake *Oligodon dorsalis* 50cm

A pretty, rather small, ground-dwelling kukri snake from north-eastern India. Head small; colour and pattern variable, the dorsum generally dark brown or purple, with a light vertebral stripe, sometimes dark-edged, or containing small black spots; a second stripe along the 2nd and 3rd dorsal scale rows; top of tail with 2–3 large black spots; forehead dark brown with two cross-bars; belly orange. Inhabits low hills in evergreen forests and is diurnal. Kukri snakes are not venomous, but need to be handled with care on account of their long, blade-like teeth that can inflict slashing bites. Nothing is known of its diet and breeding. Besides Meghalaya and Nagaland, in north-eastern India, this snake is known from Bangladesh, Bhutan, Myanmar and Thailand.

**Streaked Kukri Snake** *Oligodon taeniolata* 59cm

A familiar species of kukri snake from the hills and plains of India. A small snake; body somewhat cylindrical and stout; scales smooth; dorsum coloration variable, and typically light brown, with narrow, black, transverse cross-bars that may form irregular spots, with or without 4 dark brown, longitudinal stripes; a cream vertebral stripe sometimes present; belly cream. Found in thinly forested areas, and often enters human habitation. Active during the day as well as at dusk, this is a terrestrial species. The blade-like teeth are adaptive for cutting shells of reptile eggs, and small lizards and frogs eggs are also consumed. Between 3–9 eggs are produced in late June. Widespread in northern and peninsular India, this species also occurs in Pakistan and Sri Lanka.

**Mandalay Kukri Snake** *Oligodon theobaldi* 39cm

Dong Lin/California Academy of Sciences

A Myanmar species of kukri snake that enter our limits in the extreme north-east. A small snake; body somewhat cylindrical and stout; head short, blunt; scales smooth; dorsally light brown, with narrow, closely-set transverse or angular dark cross-bars; 4 dark, longitudinal stripes along the back; belly yellow, with or without squarish, black spots at the outer margins of the ventrals. Found in forested mid-hills as well as in the plains. Nothing is known of its diet or reproductive biology. Known only from Meghalaya State in north-eastern India, the range of the species includes Myanmar.

### Mock Viper *Psammodynastes pulverulentus* 55cm

A feisty, little, ground-dwelling or semi-arboreal snake that bites readily. Head flattened; eyes large with vertically elliptical pupil; dorsal scales smooth, lacking apical pits; dorsum coloration ranges from reddish brown to yellowish grey, to black, with small dark spots or streaks; typically, a longitudinal stripe along mid-dorsal region and three longitudinal stripes along flanks, commencing from forehead; belly spotted with brown or grey and with dark spots or longitudinal lines. Inhabits low to middle altitude forests and is terrestrial, but climbs low bushes. Usually active at dawn and at dusk, as well as at night, but daytime activity also known. Teeth are modified for feeding on heavily-scaled vertebrates, such as skinks. Frogs, geckos and the occasional small snake are also consumed. Ovoviviparous, producing 3–10 young several times a year. Northern and north-eastern India (with an isolated record from Simlipal in northern Orissa), Nepal, east to mainland and insular south-east Asia, including the Philippines.

### Pakistani Ribbon Snake *Psammophis leithii* 77cm

A striped, ground-dwelling snake from deserts and other arid habitats. Head elongated, narrow, distinct from neck, body cylindrical, rather slender; eyes large, with rounded pupils; dorsum yellowish brown, yellowish grey or straw-coloured, usually with four dark brown, longitudinal stripes, the two median ones distinct and bordered with black spots that may be contiguous, extending up to the eyes; the outer pair, when present, extend forward to the nostrils; belly unpatterned yellowish cream. Inhabits marshes, clay-like or sandy deserts and grasslands, and is generally associated with bushes, into which they retreat when alarmed. Diurnal, climbing bushes and low trees. Diet comprises skinks, and prey is constricted. Reproductive habits unknown, although young ones emerge between late September and December. Known from northern India, including Kashmir, Gujarat, Rajasthan, northern Maharashtra and Punjab States, as well as adjacent Pakistan.

## Large-eyed False Cobra *Pseudoxenodon macrops* 1.16m

A mimic of the venomous cobra, this non-venomous snake flattens its raised neck in threat. A medium-sized species; head distinct from neck; eyes large with rounded pupils; scales keeled; dorsum brownish grey, red, or olivaceous, with a series of yellow, reddish-brown or orange, dark-edged cross-bars or spots and a dorso-lateral series of dark spots; nape with a chevron-shaped, dark marking pointing forward; belly yellow, with large quadrangular, dark spots or cross-bars. Inhabits middle elevation forests of the Himalayas, and is terrestrial. Diet comprises frogs and lizards. Oviparous, producing up to 10 eggs. Distributed in eastern and north-eastern India, in addition to Nepal, east to southern China and Indo-China.

## Indian Rat Snake *Ptyas mucosa* 3.70m

A large, rat-eating snake. Eyes large with rounded pupil; scales smooth; dorsum coloration yellowish brown, olivaceous brown to black; posterior of body with dark bands or reticulate pattern; belly greyish white or yellow. Inhabits many forest types, and abundant in agricultural fields, as well as deserts, scrubland, mangroves and parks. Forages both diurnally and nocturnally. Combat dances of this species are frequently reported, when two males are partially entwined, with the forebodies raised. Diet comprises rats, and also frogs, bats, birds, lizards, turtles and other snakes. It produces a variety of sounds, from a hiss to a low growl. Clutches comprise 5–18 eggs, 51–57mm, the females guarding the eggs. Incubation period 60 days and hatchlings measure 36–47cm. Widespread in India, and distributed from Turkmenistan, through Pakistan, Nepal, Sri Lanka, Bhutan, Bangladesh, east to southern China and south-east Asia.

**Himalayan Keelback** *Rhabdophis himalayanus* 1.25m

A brightly-coloured species which is suspected of being dangerous on account of its enlarged back fangs. Eyes large with rounded pupils; dorsal scales keeled; dorsum olive to olive-brown or dark brown, with two dorso-lateral rows of widely separated, orange-yellow spots; front portion of body chequered with vermilion spots; neck with a bright yellow or orange collar, usually edged with black; a black stripe from eye to back of mouth; a black subocular stripe; belly yellowish white, becoming darker towards the tip. Inhabits forests, particularly rocky slopes, and sometimes also agricultural fields and the vicinity of streams. Diet comprises frogs, lizards and, occasionally, fish. A back-fanged snake. Oviparous. Distributed over eastern and north-eastern India, in addition to Nepal, east to Myanmar, China and Indo-China.

**Red-necked Keelback** *Rhabdophis subminiatus* 1.30m

Another brightly coloured, medium-sized snake that needs to be handled with caution. Head is distinct from neck; eyes large with rounded pupil; dorsal scales strongly keeled; anal is divided; scales are strongly keeled; dorsum olive-brown or green, un-patterned or with black and yellow reticulation; nape with yellow and red band; a dark oblique bar below eye; belly yellow, sometimes with a black dot on outer end of each shield; juveniles with a black cross-bar or triangular mark on nape, bordered with yellow behind. Inhabits forests in hill areas as well as lowlands, in the vicinity of ponds and streams. Active both during the day and at night, and terrestrial as well as semi-arboreal. A specialized eater of frogs and toads. A rear-fanged snake with venom gland, the bite of this species should be treated seriously, as the chewing action can produce life-threatening bites. Females lay 5–17 eggs, measuring 11–15 × 18–27mm, that hatch in 50 days. Hatchlings are 13–19cm in length. Several clutches may be produced in a year, and females are known to guard the eggs. Known from north-eastern India, as well as Nepal and southern China and mainland south-east Asia.

## Collared Black-headed Snake *Sibynophis subpunctatus* 76cm

A ground-dwelling, dark-collared snake. Head slightly distinct from neck; eyes large with rounded pupil; dorsal scales smooth; dorsally brown or greyish brown, with a series of black vertebral dots; a dark cross-bar behind the eyes and one on forehead; black transverse band on nape bordered posteriorly with yellow; belly yellow, each ventral with an outer black spot. Inhabits forests, both in the hills and the plains. Diurnal and terrestrial, its diet comprises skinks, snakes, frogs as well as insects. Oviparous, laying clutches of up to 6. Himalayas as far west as Shimla, to Nepal, Myanmar and south to the Malay Peninsula.

## Duméril's Black-headed Snake *Sibynophis sagittaria* 305cm

A ground-dwelling, dark-collared snake. Head slightly distinct from neck; eyes large with rounded pupil; dorsal scales smooth; dorsally brown or greyish brown, with a black, vertebral stripe; a dark cross-bar behind the eyes and one on forehead; black transverse band on nape bordered posteriorly with yellow; belly yellow, each ventral with an outer black spot. Inhabits forests. Diurnal and terrestrial, its diet comprises skinks, snakes, frogs and insects. Oviparous, laying clutches of up to 6. Known from the Himalayas as far west as Shimla, to Nepal, Myanmar and south to the Malay Peninsula.

## Black-headed Royal Snake *Spalerosophis atriceps* 1.98m

A brightly coloured snake from the dry plains of the west. Head long, with a short, truncated snout; dorsum variable in colour and pattern, typically pale yellow or orange to dusky pink, with irregular black flecks; head red, mottled with black, deep red on nape and sides of head; belly pinkish red, sometimes with dark grey mottlings. Inhabits deserts, scrub forests, rocky biotope, including old buildings. Nocturnal. Clutches of 3–8 eggs, laid in October, measuring 16–27 × 56–78mm. Restricted to north and west India, Pakistan and Nepal.

## Darjeeling Slender Snake *Trachischium fuscum* 70cm

A small snake with a short, cylindrical body, from the mid-hills of the Himalayas. Head indistinct from neck; eyes small with rounded pupils; scales keeled on posterior of body and base of tail (males) or feebly keeled or smooth (females); 13 mid-dorsal scale rows; dorsum dark brown or blackish brown, iridescent, sometimes with light longitudinal streaks; belly brown or blackish brown. Juveniles light brown dorsally, with dark, longitudinal lines. Inhabits deciduous hill forests with rocky slopes in the middle altitudes of the Himalayas. Terrestrial, it hides under stones and leaf litter during the day, emerging at dusk. Probably feeds on insects and earthworms. Oviparous, producing 3–6 eggs in a clutch. Restricted to northern to eastern India, and also Nepal.

## Yellow-spotted Keelback *Xenochrophis flavipunctatus* 1.20m

A yellow-spotted water snake that can be locally abundant in eastern and north-eastern India. Body cylindrical; head slightly distinct from neck; eye with rounded pupil; dorsal scales weakly keeled anteriorly, the keels becoming more distinct posteriorly, lacking apical pits; dorsum olivaceous or greenish grey, with black spots, which, towards the posterior of body, form a reticulate pattern; head dark olive or grey, with two dark lines from eye, and an interrupted band from base of jaw across neck and two small median ones on forehead; belly green, cream or yellow, each scale with a black line on posterior edge. A lowland species, which is more aquatic than the more familiar Checkered Keelback Water Snake, inhabiting ponds, swamps and flooded rice fields. Diurnal, feeding on fish and frogs. Typically, 20–40 eggs are laid per clutch, although a clutch size of 60 is also on record. Incubation period is 43 days and hatchlings measure 12–15cm. Distributed in eastern and north-eastern India, Nepal, east to mainland south-east Asia, up to northern Peninsular Malaysia.

## Andamans Keelback Water Snake *Xenochrophis tytleri* 1.00m

A common water snake from the Andamans, this feisty snake makes an impressive display when threatened, by rearing up and expanding its throat, while trying to make lunges. Body cylindrical; eye with rounded pupil; nostril directed slightly upwards; dorsal scales strongly keeled; dorsum olive-brown, with five dark brown or black, longitudinal stripes along the body; head brown with a black stripe from eye to upper lip and from postoculars to edge of mouth. Inhabits water bodies in the plains, including fields of rice paddies and slow-moving streams and marshes. Mostly aquatic, but can also be found moving on land at night. Diet comprises fish and frogs. Clutch size is 8–87 eggs. Widespread in the archipelago of south-east Asia, including Sumatra and Java.

**Checkered Keelback Water Snake** *Xenochrophis piscator*
1.75m

The most common water snake in the region, as well as the most aggressive. Body cylindrical; eye with rounded pupil; dorsal scales strongly keeled; dorsum olive-brown, black spots arranged in 5–6 rows; head brown with a black stripe from eye to upper lip and from postoculars to edge of mouth. A water snake from the plains, abundant in waterways, such as flooded rice fields, ponds, lakes, marshes and rivers. Active both by day and at night. Fish and frogs form the typical fare. Clutches are 4–100 eggs, most commonly 30–70, measuring 15–40mm. Females guard the eggs and incubation period is 37–90 days. Hatchlings measure 11cm. Distributed from eastern Afghanistan, through Pakistan, to southern China and Thailand.

**St John's Keelback Water Snake** *Xenochrophis sanctijohannis*
71cm

A medium-sized species, rather similar to the Checkered Keelback Water Snake, and differing in showing dorsal scales only feebly keeled or nearly smooth; only the fourth upper lip scale touching the eye; pale olive dorsally, uniform or with indistinct dark spots, sometimes with a double series of cream spots along the body; lacking dark transverse neck stripes; belly unpatterned cream. Abundant in the vicinity of agricultural fields, and more terrestrial than the Checkered Keelback. Feeds on small mammals and fish; its reproductive habits are unknown. Besides India, this species has been recorded from Pakistan and Nepal.

**Triangle-backed Water Snake** *Xenochrophis trianguligerus*
1.20m

A brightly-coloured, frog-eating water snake from the Nicobar Islands. Head large; eyes rather small; tail short; scales strongly keeled; a dark snake, ground colour of dorsum blackish brown, with orangish-red triangles on the sides of the neck and front portion of the body, the bright colours turning olive-brown or grey in older individuals; dark triangle-shaped marks on top of the body; lips cream, some scales on lips being black-edged; belly cream. Inhabits streams in lowland rainforests, as well as fields of rice paddies and the vicinity of villages. Diet comprises frogs, their eggs and larvae. Clutches of 5–15 eggs are produced at a time. Known from within Indian limits only on Great Nicobar. This species is otherwise widespread in mainland south-east Asia, besides Borneo and Sumatra.

**Günther's Narrow-headed Snake** *Xylophis stenorhynchus*
23cm

A little known, fossorial snake from the forest floor of the Western Ghats. Head indistinct from neck, snout pointed; mid dorsal scale rows 15; body cylindrical; eye moderate, with pupil either rounded or vertically elliptical; dorsal scales smooth, lacking apical pits; tail short; dorsum dark brown, unpatterned or with three darker longitudinal stripes and a yellow collar; belly unpatterned dark brown. Found in the leaf litter, in such places as buttresses of trees, within evergreen forests. Nothing is known of its diet or reproductive habits. Restricted to the Western Ghats, from the Anaimalai Hills to Tirunelveli, in Kerala and western Tamil Nadu States.

# ELAPIDAE (COBRAS AND KRAITS)

Cobras, coral snakes and kraits represent a family of snakes that have fixed fangs and produce neurotoxic venom, whose bite causes respiratory failure. India is rich in species of cobras and kraits, with several endemic species. Cobras are primarily rat eaters, while kraits and coral snakes may feed on other snakes.

**Indian Krait** *Bungarus caeruleus* 1.75m

(Top) *South-east coast population;* (above) *south-west coast population*

A medium-sized, terrestrial snake that is dangerous to humans and responsible for a large number of mortalities. Head indistinct from neck; body cylindrical; eyes small; scales shiny; vertebral scales enlarged; hexagonal; dorsum steely-blue, black or dark brown with paired narrow white bands across the body; belly unpatterned cream. Widespread in the plains, in thinly wooded forests, agricultural fields as well as the edges of human habitation. Nocturnal when foraging, it hides under piles of debris at other times. During the day, it is non-aggressive, flattening the body, and attempting to hide its head under its body; at night, it may bite without provocation. Snakes are the almost exclusive item in the diet of kraits, although mice, frogs and lizards are occasionally taken. Cannibalism is on record. Mating takes place between February and March. Oviparous, laying 6–15 eggs, measuring 19 × 35mm that are guarded by the females. Eggs hatch between May and July, hatchlings measure 27–30cm. The fangs are rather short, and the venom highly toxic, causing respiratory failure. Widespread from Afghanistan, Pakistan, Nepal, Sri Lanka and Nepal.

**Banded Krait** *Bungarus fasciatus* 2.25m

An unmistakable dark- and light-banded snake. Body triangular in cross-section; tail short and stumpy; dorsum with alternating black and yellow bands that are approximately equal in size; and top of head with a V-shaped marking. Inhabits lowlands, in lightly forested areas, swamps and the vicinity of villages. Although timid and non-aggressive by day, it is a highly venomous snake, and is known to become bold by night. A snake-eating species, it eats water snakes, rat snakes, pythons and vine snakes, besides lizards, frogs and fish. Clutches comprise 4–14 eggs that are produced in April, which hatch after an incubation period of 61 days, hatchlings 25–30cm. Widespread in eastern and north-eastern India, the range includes south-east Asia.

**Black Krait** *Bungarus niger* 1.20m

Frank Tillack

An extremely venomous land snake from the eastern Himalayas and north-eastern India. Head indistinct from neck; eye rather small, with rounded pupil; scales smooth; vertebral scales enlarged; all subcaudals are single; dorsum black or bluish black; belly as well as undersurface of tail cream with dark mottlings. Nothing is known of the diet and reproductive habits of this species. Restricted to northern West Bengal, Assam and Meghalaya States, as well as Nepal.

## MacClelland's Coral Snake *Sinomicrurus macclellandi* 84cm

A brightly coloured snake that advertises its deadly bite. Head short and rounded; body cylindrical; scales smooth; subcaudals typically divided; dorsum reddish brown, with 23–40 thin, black stripes that are light-edged; tail with 2–6 black bands; belly yellowish cream with black marks. Inhabits the forest floor in lowland forests and in the hills at altitudes of 900–1,800m. Nocturnal, it feeds on snakes and lizards. Females lay 6–14 eggs in a clutch. Besides north-eastern India, this species occurs in Nepal, Bangladesh, eastern China, Myanmar, Vietnam, Laos and Thailand.

## Black Slender Coral Snake *Calliophis nigrescens* 1.14m

A very elongate, dark coral snake from the hill ranges of Peninsular India. Head not distinct from neck; eye rather small; dorsum coloration variable, and may be reddish brown to green or purplish brown, with 3–5 black stripes, with or without black edges; forehead with or without darker markings; belly unpatterned red. Inhabits mountains at elevations of 900–2,100m. A fossorial snake, whose diet is entirely comprised of other snakes. Reproductive habits unknown. Although venomous, with presumably a neurotoxic venom, there are no recorded cases of human mortalities from its bite. Distributed patchily along the entire length of the Western Ghats, from the Satpura Dangs of Gujarat State, down through Panchgani, Anaimalai, to the Nilgiri and Travancore Hills, as well as the Shevaroy Hills of Kerala and western Tamil Nadu States.

## Monocled Cobra *Naja kaouthia* 2.30m

A dangerously venomous snake that is responsible for a large number of human mortalities annually, and usually identifiable by the monocle-like marking on the expanded hood. Head distinct from body; dorsum brown, greyish brown or blackish brown; some with darker bands; hood marking typically a light circle with a dark centre; the light throat colour extends less far back than in the Spectacled Cobra. Inhabits the wetter parts of the region, compared to its close relative, and is known from agricultural fields and plantations, as well as forests, occasionally entering areas of human habitation. Typically crepuscular and some populations are

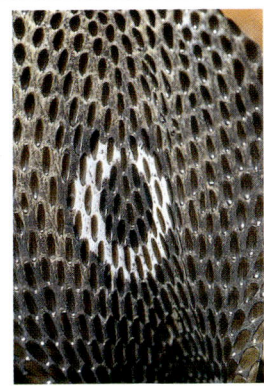

*Hood*

capable of spitting their neurotoxic venom. Rodents, frogs and, occasionally, fish and other snakes are eaten. Clutches of 15–30 eggs are laid between January and March, with the female guarding the nest during the incubation period, which is about 50 days. Distributed along northern to north-eastern India, the range includes Nepal and Bangladesh, and extends to eastern China and mainland south-east Asia, up to the northern part of Peninsular Malaysia.

## Spectacled Cobra *Naja naja* 2.20m

A dangerously venomous snake responsible for many human mortalities, identifiable by the spectacle-like marking on the hood. Dorsum greyish brown or brown-black, some populations from western India jet black, without any hood markings; hood marking typically a light spectacle. Inhabits the dry parts of the region, from plantations and forests, occasionally entering human habitation. Crepuscular, diurnal or nocturnal, with neurotoxic venom that causes respiratory failure. Rodents comprise the mainstay of the diet; frogs, birds, lizards, eggs of birds, fish and snakes are also consumed.

*Hood*

Clutches of 12–30 eggs laid between April and July; the eggs hatch after about 60 days. Hatchlings 20–30cm. Distributed northern to eastern India, up to western Assam State; also Pakistan, Nepal, Bhutan, Sri Lanka and, possibly, Afghanistan.

## Central Asian Cobra *Naja oxiana* 1.50m

Another dangerously venomous snake, although not of great medicinal importance, it is identifiable by the lack of a distinct marking on the expanded hood. Dorsum of juveniles distinctly banded, disappearing with growth, ground colour dark brown, and usually not black, no hood markings, although the banding on the dorsum may continue on to the hood. Inhabits arid and semi-arid regions, as well as in relatively damp grasslands and agricultural areas, up to an altitude of 1,500m. Venom neurotoxic, although bites are rare. Diurnal during most parts of the year, except during the summer, when they become crepuscular. Rodents, frogs and lizards form the diet of this species. Hatchlings appear between June and July, and measure 30–35cm. In India, this species is restricted to Jammu and Kashmir, the range of the species extending from Central Asia, through Afghanistan to Pakistan.

## Andaman Cobra *Naja sagittifera* 64cm

(Above) *Full body;* (left) *hood*

A potentially dangerously venomous snake, also not of medicinal importance, this is endemic of the Andaman Islands. It is identifiable by a monocled pattern on the expanded hood. Head distinct from body; dorsum shiny black in adults, with light chevron-shaped markings in juveniles; a monocle-like marking on the hood, comprising a light circle with a dark centre; throat grey and belly grey. Inhabits forested areas and plantations in the plains. Nothing is known of its venom, which is presumably neurotoxic. Its diet and reproductive biology remain unknown, although captives are known to accept rodents. Restricted to the Andaman Islands in the Bay of Bengal, this species may have the smallest range known for a cobra.

# King Cobra *Ophiophagus hannah* 5.5m

Nikolai Lyuzianovich Orlov

The largest venomous snake. As there are not one but several species hidden within this complex, there is a great diversity in coloration, scalation and body proportion noticeable. Dorsum of body dark brown, olive-brown or grey-black, with pale yellow or orange bands in young that may or may not persist in adults. A pair of large occipital scales. Terrestrial as well as arboreal. King Cobras feed on other snakes and, occasionally, on monitor lizards. Females construct a mound nest by collecting fallen leaves, in which eggs are deposited and guarded. Clutches comprise 24 eggs and incubation period is 63 days. Hatchlings 29–42cm. There are a few authenticated cases of attacks on humans. The enormous venom glands of the King Cobra contain enough venom to kill even an elephant. Known from the Himalayan foothills, south-western, north-eastern India, east to Indo-China and Indo-Malaya, up to Sulawesi in Indonesia.

## HYDROPHIIDAE (SEA SNAKES)

True sea snakes can be easily differentiated from all other families of snakes, even when they enter salt water, by the flattened, paddle-like tails and short fangs at the back of their upper jaws. Further, sea snakes are completely aquatic and produce live young, never coming ashore, with the exception of the sea kraits, that bask, rest and lay eggs on small islands. Although mostly marine, some travel upriver, in tidal portions of rivers. They have fixed fangs, like cobras and kraits, and their bite is extremely venomous, although, due to the generally inaccessible nature of their habitats and their usually non-aggressive nature, few people are bitten.

### Hook-nosed Sea Snake *Enhydrina schistosus* 1.50m

An aggressive sea snake responsible for some human casualties. Scales distinctly keeled and rostral scale on upperjaw gives it a beak-like appearance; dorsum of body and forehead greyish olive; body with indistinct darker markings. Feeds on marine catfishes. Ovoviviparous; 4–11 young produced December to February, 25–28cm long. Widespread along east coast of India.

## Annulated Sea Snake *Hydrophis cyanocinctus* 1.90m

A small sea snake, with strongly keeled scales. Head is small and almost indistinct from neck, the body thickening towards the posterior; colour and pattern variable; dorsum typically olive or yellow, with darker transverse bands that may or may not encircle the body; belly yellowish cream. The diet of this species includes fish, especially eels, and also marine invertebrates. Clutches comprise 3–16 young, measuring 38cm. Widespread in coastal parts of the Indian mainland, distribution extends from the Persian Gulf, east to include south-east Asia and Japan.

## Banded Sea Snake *Laticauda colubrina* 1.70m

A very common sea snake from rocky islands of the Bay. A robust species, with rounded pupils and a flat tail. This is a dark-light banded species, the black annuli numbering 36–50, and are separated by bluish-grey bands. Adult males are much smaller than females. A non-aggressive species, it should none the less be handled with caution on account of its toxic venom, and deaths from its bite are on record. It comes ashore, to lay eggs, bask, rest and perhaps also to digest food. Diet comprises eels. Eggs are produced in caves on rocky islands, between June and August. Clutches are 3–13, measuring 20–31 × 45–92mm. Known from the Andaman and Nicobar Islands, and there are also a few isolated records from the coasts of the Indian mainland, the range of the species extending all the way to the South Pacific.

# LEPTOTYPHLOPIDAE (THREAD SNAKES)

Rather similar to the blind snakes are thread snakes, which are also fossorial, worm-like snakes, but restricted to drier areas, and have even more elongated bodies. Worms and insects form the diet of these snakes.

**Large-beaked Thread Snake** *Leptotyphlops macrorhynchus*
28cm

A long, thin, fossorial snake from the drier western parts. Head indistinct from body; upper-jaw protruding over lower-jaw; eyes distinct; scales smooth; dorsum pinkish brown, eyes dark. Inhabits stony and other arid regions, where they hide under stones, venturing out during the wet season, when they enter gardens. Diet comprises termites. North-western India, distribution extending to the Middle East.

# TYPHLOPIDAE (BLIND SNAKES)

Worm-like in external appearance, blind snakes are burrowers, living under the soil and in the leaf litter. They frequently appear during the rains, when they are flooded out of their subterranean haunts. Worms, ants, termites and their larvae form their dietary mainstay.

**Brahminy Blind Snake** *Ramphotyphlops braminus* 17.5cm

A small, worm-like snake, that occasionally enters houses. Eyes distinct; tail terminates in a spine; dorsally, black or brown, belly lighter; snout and tip of tail paler. Usually encountered in the soil or crawling on wet soil surface. Diet comprises termites, ants, their larvae and earthworms. This species has been spread worldwide accidentally in flower pots, and is parthenogenetic, producing eggs without mating. Widespread in tropical and subtropical regions of Asia.

## Large Blind Snake *Typhlops diardii* 43cm

Mark O'Shea

A very large species of blind snake, widely distributed along the foothills of the Himalayas, and across north-eastern India, to south-east Asia. Eyes visible; dorsum dark brown, each scale with a indistinct light transverse streak; belly and sides light brown. Fossorial, inhabiting the soil, in rotting logs or under debris. Diet comprises insects and earthworms. Either ovoviviparous or oviparous with a long egg-retention time, producing up to 14 live young at a time. Besides the Indian region, it is known from Myanmar, Thailand and Peninsular Malaysia.

## Jerdon's Blind Snake *Typhlops jerdoni* 28cm

Perhaps the commonest blind snake in the eastern Himalayas. Snout rounded; eye distinct; tail bluntly pointed, ending in a tiny spine, which is cream-coloured below; dark brown to nearly black above; belly light brown; snout and anal region cream. Abundant locally, and found under boulders and rocks and inside dead trees, presumably where their food – termites and earthworms – are common. Known from Sikkim and northern West Bengal, as well as Arunachal Pradesh and Meghalaya States, with isolated records from Bhutan and Myanmar.

# UROPELTIDAE (SHIELDTAILED SNAKES)

Shieldtailed snakes are so called for the flat scale at the tip of their tails, resembling a shield. They are restricted to Peninsular India, particularly the Western Ghats, and the central and associated hill ranges of Sri Lanka. They are burrowers, feeding on soft-bodied invertebrates. Many species are brightly coloured, with smooth, iridescent scales.

### Madurai Shieldtail *Platyplectrurus madurensis* 44cm

S. U. Saravanakumar

A purple-coloured shieldtailed snake. Body slender; snout obtuse; scales smooth; tail shield flat, with two ridges meeting at a point; dorsum unpatterned purplish brown above; belly with 1–2 scale rows white-centred. Fossorial, inhabiting forests and gardens at elevations of 1,200–1,800m. Ovoviviparous, producing 4–5 young in June and July. Palni and Travancore Hills of Tamil Nadu and Kerala.

### Ashambu Shieldtail *Uropeltis liura* 32cm

A small, slender-bodied shieldtail. Snout acute; scales smooth; dorsum purplish brown; a transverse series of small, yellow, black-edged ocelli; belly with large, alternating black and yellow spots or crossbars. Fossorial, preferring clayey-humus soil, and burrows to 30cm, in gardens as well as edges of cardamom plantations. Ovoviviparous, four young born between May and June. Tirunelveli Hills and adjacent Kerala in southern Western Ghats, between 135–1,500m.

**Large-scaled Shieldtail** *Uropeltis macrolepis* 30cm

A relatively common species of shieldtailed snake from the hills of Maharashtra. Snout rounded; tip of tail truncated obliquely; tail shield large, with small spines; dorsum black or dark purplish brown, scales light-margined; a short yellow or orange stripe on lips and sides of neck; a broad, yellow or orange stripe along the tail; belly black or purplish brown. Fossorial and seen on the surface during the wet season. Diet presumably comprises earthworms and insects, and nothing is known of its breeding habits. Restricted to the northern portion of the Western Ghats, near Mumbai, in Maharashtra State.

## VIPERIDAE (VIPERS AND PIT VIPERS)

Vipers represent the most specialized of the venomous snakes, capable of delivering their venom through enlarged fangs that are foldable and hollow. Their venom is haemotoxic, affecting the blood, and a bite from one of the larger species, such as the Russell's Viper is excruciatingly painful. Pit vipers have sensory pits on the snout, that act as thermal detectors for locating warm-bodied prey.

**Russell's Viper** *Daboia russelii* 1.85m

A thick-set, ground-dwelling viper. Nostril large; dorsum brown, with three rows of spots along body, a dark brown one along midline, and a blackish-brown or black one on each side; belly cream. Terrestrial, crepuscular. Inhabits grasslands, scrub forests and open forests. Diet comprises rodents, crabs, frogs, lizards and birds. The haemotoxic venom causes intense burning pain, swelling and discoloration. Ovoviviparous, clutch size 6–63 produced between May and July. Widespread in the plains of India. Also, Pakistan, Bangladesh, Sri Lanka, east to south-east Asia.

**Saw-scaled Viper** *Echis carinatus* 30cm (Peninsular India)/80cm (northern India)

This small snake accounts for a large percentage of mortalities from snake-bite. Head oval, slightly distinct from neck, the body frequently coiled up in a resting position. On loose substrate, such as sand, it uses sidewinding movement to proceed. When threatened, they rub their scales, producing a rasping sound. Diet includes mice, squirrels, lizards, snakes, frogs, locusts and centipedes. Clutches of 3–4 or 10–19 young, depending on locality, produced between May and June, neonates measuring 9–13mm. Venom haemotoxic, causing burning pain. The distribution of the species extends to the Middle East.

**Himalayan Pit Viper** *Gloydius himalayanus* 86cm

A large-growing pit viper from the high Himalayas, this may be the snake found at the greatest altitude on earth – at 4,877m. Head somewhat flattened, distinct from neck, deep sensory pits between eye and nostril; mid-dorsal scale rows 21, dorsum brown, with darker patterns, typically with 23–45 cross-bars demarcated by their darker edges. A slow-moving, nocturnal pit viper, it is generally non-aggressive and is not of medical importance. Inhabits forested habitats from 1,524m in alpine regions of the western and central Himalayas. Small rodents and skinks, as well as centipedes, constitute the diet of the species, and are sometimes captured by caudal luring, whereby the bright yellow tail tip is slowly waved. Reproductive season is between July and September, when 3–7 young are born, measuring 10–16cm. Widely distributed, in northern India from Kashmir, through Haryana, Himachal Pradesh, Uttar Pradesh and possibly the Sikkim States, and also in Nepal, northern Pakistan and possibly Afghanistan.

**Hump-nosed Pit Viper** *Hypnale hypnale* 55cm

A short, relatively stout species of pit viper, abundant in the hill ranges of the Western Ghats. Head distinct from neck; snout upturned; pupil of eye vertically elliptical; coloration variable, and ranging in ground colour from light brown to blackish brown, stippled with grey and brown; a series of 20–33 oval or triangular marks present at the sides, meeting at the vertebral region; a dark cheek stripe from eye to jaws; tail with dark crossbands. Found in leaf litter, buttresses of trees, rocks or on low vegetation, within evergreen and moist deciduous forests. When threatened, it vibrates its tail. Small vertebrates, such as geckos and rodents form the diet. The breeding season of this live-bearing species is between March and July, when 4–17 young are produced, measuring 13–14.5cm. Restricted to the Western Ghats of India, from Karnataka, through western Tamil Nadu and Kerala States, and also central Sri Lanka.

**Blotched Pit Viper** *Ovophis monticola* 1.15m

A stout, ground-dwelling species of pit viper from eastern and north-eastern India. Head broad; distinct from neck; eyes relatively small; pupil vertically elliptical; dorsal scales smooth; tail not prehensile; dorsum brownish grey or yellowish pink; with dark brown blotches; forehead is darker. A montane forest species, distributed along the middle altitudes of the Himalayas. Nocturnal and terrestrial. Venomous, although not of medicinal importance. Diet includes warm-blooded prey, such as rats and mice. An oviparous species, unlike the common pit vipers, laying 5–18 spherical eggs measuring 18–20mm. Known from the eastern and north-eastern parts of India, in addition to Bangladesh and Nepal, extending to southern China, Myanmar and Thailand. Populations from other parts of south-east Asia once referred to this species should be considered distinct.

## Jerdon's Pit Viper *Protobothrops jerdoni* 99cm

A fairly large, ground-dwelling pit viper from north-eastern India. Snout relatively long; forehead scales reduced; scales strongly keeled; dorsum greenish yellow or olive, with a series of reddish-brown blotches that are edged with black; forehead black, with fine, yellow lines; upper lip yellow; belly yellow, spotted with black. Inhabits montane forests, with evergreen vegetation and is nocturnal. Diet is unknown, and presumably comprises small rodents and birds. Ovoviviparous, producing 4–8 young between August and September. Known from the Khasi Hills of Meghalaya State, as well as southern China and northern Myanmar.

## Brown-spotted Pit Viper *Protobothrops mucrosquamatus* 1.16m

Another large, ground-dwelling pit viper from north-eastern India. Head relatively elongated; forehead scales reduced; scales strongly keeled; dorsum greyish olive or brown, with a series of large brown spots with dark edges; head sometimes with a dark streak on the sides; tail light brown, with black spots; belly cream, with light brown speckles. Oviparous, laying 5–13 eggs at a time. Known from Nagaland and Arunachal Pradesh, besides Bangladesh, and further east, from southern China, Myanmar and northern Vietnam.

**White-lipped Pit Viper** *Cryptelytrops albolabris* 1.04m

A thick, green pit viper with distinct white lips. Head relatively long, narrower than neck; body stout; small scales on forehead; dorsal scales keeled; tail prehensile; eyes yellow; head and dorsum green; males with a white stripe on the first row of dorsal scales, which is indistinct or absent in females; belly green or yellowish cream. Inhabits forests, generally in the vicinity of streams. Nocturnal and found on vegetation, such as trees and saplings, and occasionally, on the ground. Aggressive, and bites freely, although human mortalities are rare. Diet comprises mice, birds, lizards and frogs. Ovoviviparous, producing 7–16 young at a time, 12–18cm long. Distributed from north-eastern India, in addition to Nepal and Bangladesh, east to southern China, and the mainland and islands of south-east Asia.

**Anderson's Pit Viper** *Cryptelytrops andersoni* 1.10m

A common, brown pit viper from the Andaman Islands. Head distinct from neck; snout relatively long; scales on forehead not tuberculate; dorsal scales strongly keeled; dorsum coloration as well as pattern variable, and typically has brown variegations on an olive ground colour; belly pale brown. Inhabits lowland rainforests as well as clearings within villages and the edges of agricultural fields. Nocturnal, it sits in wait for small rodents and geckos at the edges of forest trails and on the leaf litter. Reproductive habits unknown. Bites are common, but human mortalities have not been recorded. Restricted to the Andaman Islands.

## Cantor's Pit Viper *Cryptelytrops cantori* 1.15m

A pit viper restricted in distribution to a tiny island of the central Nicobars. Head distinct from neck; snout relatively long; forehead scales smooth or weakly keeled; dorsal scales smooth or weakly keeled; dorsum coloration and pattern variable, and may be olive or light or dark brown, with or without darker brown or yellow spots; a cream line along the eyes; another line of the same colour along the sides of the body; belly cream or green; the undersurface of the tail brown-spotted. Known from the vicinity of human habitation and is nocturnal, presumably feeding on birds and small mammals. Human fatalities from the bite of this species are on record. Known only from Kamorta Island, which is part of the Central Nicobars Archipelago.

## Green Pit Viper *Trimeresurus gramineus* 80cm

A green pit viper from Peninsular India. Small scales on forehead; dorsal scales weakly keeled; tail prehensile; eyes yellow; head and dorsum green or greenish yellow, sometimes with dark brown blotches; upper lips cream; belly pale green or yellowish cream. Inhabits forested areas, including bamboo groves. Nocturnal and arboreal, frequently found at edges of streams. Aggressive, and bites freely, although human mortalities are rare. Diet comprises lizards and birds. Clutch size is 6–20, and hatchlings are 12cm in length, bright green in colour, with a dark streak on each side of head, back with dark cross-bars. Restricted to Peninsular India, especially along the broken hill range along the east coast.

**Large-scaled Pit Viper** *Peltopelor macrolepis* 58cm

A large-scaled, bright-green pit viper. Snout relatively long; forehead scales enlarged; smooth; tail prehensile. These snakes are dark grey in the wet season, light yellowish grey in the dry season; belly pale green. An inhabitant of evergreen forests and sometimes also tea gardens. Diet consists of rodents. Clutch sizes are 4–7, produced in October. Tea-pickers are often bitten by this pit viper, but the bites are rarely fatal. Known from the southern ranges of the Western Ghats in the states of Kerala and western Tamil Nadu.

**Malabar Pit Viper** *Trimeresurus malabaricus* 1.05m

A large species of pit viper from the Western Ghats and Shevaroy Hills. Head relatively long, narrower than neck; body stout; small scales on forehead; dorsal scales weakly keeled; tail prehensile; head and dorsum olive or brownish olive, with a series of black or dark brown spots that are often fused to form a zig-zag pattern; sides yellow-spotted; sides of head with a black streak; tail with black and yellow variegations; belly pale green or yellowish cream. The coloration changes seasonally, being light in the dry season and dark in the wet one. Inhabits moist deciduous and evergreen forests, at altitudes of 600–2,100m. Nocturnal and found on low vegetation, shrubs or on the ground. Aggressive, and bites freely, and given its large-size bites should be treated seriously. The diet of this large pit viper includes geckos, tree frogs and musk shrews. Widespread along the hill ranges from Maharashtra, Goa, Karnataka, Kerala and western Tamil Nadu States.

## Medo Pit Viper *Viridovipera medoensis* 56cm

A green, arboreal pit viper from north-eastern India. Head flattened, triangular, distinct from neck; scales on upper snout enlarged; long, prehensile tail; dorsum dark green, sometimes edged with turquoise blue, with a bicoloured white/red ventrolateral stripe; belly lighter green. Inhabits tropical and subtropical montane forests, 1,000–1,400 m. Arboreal and nocturnal, associated with bamboo forests, and hibernating November to April. Diet consists of frogs and small mammals, such as rodents. A potentially dangerous snake, although no cases of human mortality are known. Found in Arunachal Pradesh, in north-eastern India, China and northern Myanmar.

## Pope's Pit Viper *Popeia popeiorum* 1.00m

A green pit viper from montane regions. A relatively slender species; head small and flat; dorsal scales either smooth or weakly keeled; dorsum bright green or pale green, a white line runs along the length of the body and tail; belly light green; tail reddish brown. Arboreal, nocturnal in habit, occurring in high montane and submontane forests. When threatened, it vibrates its tail-tip. Its venom is neurotoxic and known to cause human casualties. Diet consists of birds, frogs, lizards, rats and squirrels. Ovoviviparous, clutches of 10 being produced from April to May; new born 18cm. Known from north-eastern India, with range extending into south-east Asia.

### Stejneger's Pit Viper *Viridovipera stejnegeri* 1.12m

Another green species of pit viper, this one is named for the American herpetologist, Leonhardt Stejneger, and has reddish-brown eyes and is very similar superficially to Pope's Pit Viper and differentiable in showing a different hemipenis shape. Head large, distinct from neck; dorsum and head bright green; ventrum pale or greenish cream; males typically with a white stripe behind the eyes; another stripe of the same colour bordered at the bottom with red or orange, runs along the side of the body. Inhabits hill forests, up to an altitude of 2,845m, and forages at night on bushes and low trees. A dangerous snake, owing to its relatively large body size and potent neurotoxic venom. Diet comprises rodents, birds, lizards and frogs. Ovoviviparous, producing 3–10 young at a time. Within India, this species is restricted to the northeast, but the range of the species also includes Myanmar, Cambodia, Vietnam, Thailand and southern China.

## XENOPELTIDAE (SUNBEAM SNAKES)

The two living species of this family look like living holograms, with smooth, iridescent dorsal scales, short tails and cylindrical bodies. They are burrowers, with a flattened snout.

### Sunbeam Snake *Xenopeltis unicolor* 1.25m

A burrowing snake, with highly iridescent scales. Snout depressed and rounded; eyes small; tail short; dorsum iridescent brown, each scale light edged; belly white or cream. In juveniles, a pale yellow or cream collar. Inhabits swamps and lowland forests. Nocturnal and semi-fossorial, it feeds on rodents, ground-nesting birds, amphibians and other snakes. Clutches of 6–17 eggs, measure 18 × 58mm. Found on the Nicobar Islands, as well as Myanmar, south-eastern China, and south-east Asia.

# AGAMIDAE (DRAGONS)

Agamas or 'dragons' are day-active lizards, usually with a crest along the middle of their backs. Most species live on trees and bushes in forested areas; there are some that dwell on sand or on rocks. Nearly all are insectivorous, sitting in wait for appropriately sized insects or invertebrates to come within striking distance. A few supplement their diet by eating flower petals and seeds. They dig shallow nests in the earth, in which their soft-shelled eggs are deposited. These lizards range from Africa, Europe and Asia to New Guinea and Australia. Sexual dimorphism tends to be dramatic, and used in interspecific interactions. Members of the family include the flying lizards, which have evolved elongated ribs covered with skin, that permit them to glide for distances exceeding 30m.

**Lesser Agama** *Brachysaura minor* 9cm

Raju Vyas

A pot-bellied, ground-dwelling lizard from western and central India. Head large; body stout; scales keeled, dorsal ones larger than those on belly; a distinct nuchal crest, comprising a single scale; two groups of spines above tympanum; throat fold present; dorsum olive, with three rows of dark brown, light-edged spots; yellowish cream ventrally; females during the breeding season becoming bright red on the sides of the body and show a deep black throat; juveniles olive or pinkish brown, with dark brown band between eyes. Inhabits scrub forests and plains. Diet comprises seeds, as well as more typical agamid fare, such as earwigs, beetles, grasshoppers and spiders. A crepuscular and nocturnal lizard, it is sluggish and terrestrial, generally found sitting on stones, but can climb up to a metre on vegetation. Clutch size is 8–10. When alarmed, they emit a squeak. Known from the western and central parts of the peninsula, including Kachchh in Gujarat, Madhya Pradesh and western Uttar Pradesh.

**Green Crested Lizard** *Bronchocela cristatella* 13cm

This is a bright green (brown when threatened) agamid from the Nicobar Islands. Head long; snout slightly longer than orbit; body distinctly compressed; dorsal crest somewhat distinct, not extending to tail; scales unequal, smooth; tympanum diameter half that of orbit; dorsum bright green; ear region brown, the entire body assuming this colour when threatened; belly cream. Diurnal and arboreal, it is capable of making short glides between trees. A forest-edge species, it also invades parks and gardens. Eggs are spindle-shaped, with pointed ends, measuring 8–11 × 30–36mm. Besides the Nicobar Islands, this species occurs in south-east Asia.

**Laungwala Toad-headed Lizard** *Bufoniceps laungwalansis* 7cm

A squat-bodied desert lizard from the deserts of Rajasthan State. It has a tiny external ear opening and deeply set tympanum, a short snout, with nostrils set close together high on snout, a depressed body with small, uniform scales; tail short and there is no dorsal crest, gular sac or femoral and preanal pores; digits bear fringes of flat, pointed scales; dorsum grey with red, orange, black and white spots, some animals showing a dark vertebral stripe. A dune-dweller, it is active in the mornings and after the heat of the day, in the late afternoons. Its diet comprises ants, beetles, grasshoppers, flies and lizards. They can burrow in loose sand by lateral movements and by shivering movements of the body, but do not excavate burrows. Restricted to the western part of Rajasthan State, in extreme western India.

## Green Forest Lizard *Calotes calotes* 13cm

A highly arboreal, bright green forest lizard, fairly widespread in the plains and mid-hills of Peninsular India. Head large; cheek swollen in adult males; crest on head and body distinct; an oblique fold in front of the shoulder; throat sac not well-developed; dorsal scales smooth or weakly keeled, pointing backwards and upwards; tail long, rounded; dorsum bright green, with 4–5 bluish-white or green cross-bars; belly pale green. Inhabits moist deciduous and evergreen forests in the mid-hills and plains, and is found on shrubs as well as tree trunks. Diet comprises insects. Clutches include 6–12 spherical, soft-shelled eggs that are laid between April to September, eggs measuring 12–13 × 18–19mm that hatch in 79–84 days. Besides Peninsular India, this species is known from Sri Lanka.

## Elliot's Forest Lizard *Calotes ellioti* 7cm

An arboreal, olive-brown forest lizard from the Western Ghats. Head rather small; cheek not swollen in adult males; crest on head and body distinct; an oblique fold in front of the shoulder; throat sac not well-developed; dorsal scales keeled, pointing backwards, and apart from the top 2–3 rows, also downwards; tail long, rounded, dorsum olive with dark brown cross-bars; an angular black mark on side of neck; a white spot below eye, which shows dark radiating lines; belly unpatterned cream. Inhabits moist deciduous and evergreen forests in the mid-hills, and is found on shrubs as well as tree trunks. Diet comprises insects. Clutch size is 3–5, eggs measuring 5 × 12mm are deposited in April. Widely distributed in the southern ranges of Anaimalai, Tirunelveli, Sivagiri and Malabar Hills of Kerala and western Tamil Nadu States.

## Large-scaled Forest Lizard *Calotes grandisquamis* 15cm

A large-scaled, green lizard from the mid-hills of the Western Ghats. Head relatively small, although a little longer than in the Nilgiri Forest Lizard; a row of three spines above tympanum; nuchal crest comprising 12 lanceolate spines; dorsal scales enlarged, pointing backwards and upwards; a fold in front of the shoulder; dorsum green, unpatterned or with broad, black, transverse bars; an orange spot frequently in the centre of each black scale within the bars; belly pale green. Inhabits the mid-hills of evergreen forests and is diurnal and insectivorous. Nesting takes place in October, after the South-west Monsoons, when 6–12 eggs are deposited in a hole, 40mm deep, excavated on the forest floor. Restricted to the southern ranges of the Anaimalai, Brahmagiri and Ponmudi, in Kerala and western Tamil Nadu States.

## Jerdon's Forest Lizard *Calotes jerdoni* 10cm

A weakly-crested, bright green forest lizard from north-eastern India. Head rather large; dorsal crest present, although nuchal crest weak; a distinct fold in front of shoulder; dorsal scales larger than ventrals; two parallel rows of compressed scales above tympanum; dorsum bright green, with a pair of black-edged, brown bands and yellow, orange or brown blotches; tail dark banded or spotted. Diurnal and arboreal, feeding on insects. Breeding takes place in August. Clutches comprise 12 eggs and hatchlings measure 7cm in total length. Known from the Khasi Hills of Meghalaya State, and also from Myanmar and southern China.

## Nilgiri Forest Lizard *Calotes nemoricola* 15cm

A medium-sized arboreal lizard with dark facial markings, from the hills of the southern Western Ghats. Head relatively small; a row of three spines above tympanum; nuchal crest comprising 12 lanceolate spines; dorsal scales enlarged, pointing backwards and upwards; a fold in front of the shoulder; dorsum changeable from bright green to greenish brown; body with three transverse, yellow bars that fail to reach the dorsal ridge; a dark patch behind the eye covering the tympanum; cheek and area above tympanum bright yellow; tail dark-banded. Inhabits evergreen forests at middle altitudes in the Western Ghats. Diurnal, active on branches and saplings above ground. Six eggs are produced in June. Restricted to the Niligiri, Ponmudi and Anaimalai Hills of the Western Ghats.

## Roux's Forest Lizard *Calotes rouxii* 8cm

A common forest-dwelling lizard from the plains and mid-hills of the Western Ghats. Head rather small; 2 slender spines on each side of the head; dark fold in front of the shoulder; throat reddish orange in both sexes; upper lip with a white or cream spot. Inhabits lowlands and the mid-hills, within deciduous and semi-evergreen forests. Diurnal, active at bases of trees, on boulders near streams and on fallen trees within evergreen forests. Diet comprises insects. Clutch size is 2–9, measuring 20mm, produced between May and September. Known from the states of Gujarat, Maharashtra, Karnataka, Kerala and western Tamil Nadu.

## Indian Garden Lizard *Calotes versicolor* 45cm

(Top) *Adult;* (above) *juvenile*

The most abundant and widespread lizard, found in parks and gardens. Head rather large; scales on body pointing backwards and upwards; 2 separated spines above tympanum; coloration variable, head becoming bright red, and a black patch on the throat appearing in displaying males, fading to dull grey at other times. Males exceed females in size, as well as showing swollen cheeks and longer dorsal spines. Diet comprises insects and other invertebrates, although unripe seeds are also consumed. Eggs laid during the summer in northern India, in the wet season in southern India. Clutches comprise 69 eggs in southern India, the largest clutch recorded in northern India being 23. Eggs 4–5 × 10–11mm and incubation period 42–67 days. Widespread in the plains of India and adjacent countries.

## Bay Islands Forest Lizard *Coryphophylax subcristatus* 10cm

Perhaps the most abundant lizard in the Andaman and Nicobar Islands, the Bay Islands Forest Lizard is found in almost every type of forested habitat. Dorsal crest present; dorsal scales small, intermixed with larger scales; preanal and femoral pores absent; cheeks swollen in adult males; ventral scales strongly keeled; dorsum brownish olive, unpatterned, spotted or striped with dark brown; juveniles more green, with dark cross-bars; belly light brown. Inhabits lowland rainforest and the plains, including the edges of mangrove forests. They are diurnal and feed on insects, and are active on trunks of trees, on saplings, as well as on the ground. A single large egg is produced at a time. Restricted to the Andaman and Nicobar Islands in the Bay of Bengal.

## Blanford's Flying Lizard *Draco blanfordi* 13cm

The only flying lizard recorded from the north-east of the country. Wing-like membrane on the sides of body; nostrils directed upwards; five ribs in the wing membrane, which has five dark transverse bands; dorsum bluish grey or brownish grey; head and shoulder with small dark spots; belly yellow; gular pouch yellowish white. Inhabits evergreen forests and is diurnal, presumably feeding on ants. Nothing is known of the breeding biology of this lizard. Reported from eastern Assam, in north-eastern India; also, Bangladesh and northern Myanmar.

## Western Ghats Flying Lizard *Draco dussumieri* 10cm

A 'winged' lizard from the Western Ghats, capable of making glides between trees. A large membrane of skin on each side of the body, supported by elongated extensions of ribs; nostril directed upwards; six ribs in flying membrane; dorsum dark brown; the membrane light brown towards the body, darker on edges, with large, light spots; belly dark grey; gular pouch yellow with dark spots in males. Inhabits evergreen, moist deciduous forests and plantations. Active by day on tree trunks, where they feed on ants. Mating takes place between February and April. Three to four eggs, 8 × 14mm, produced in July, and deposited in a hole at the base of trees. Incubation period 50 days and hatchlings 3.2cm. Restricted to Kerala, Karnataka and western Tamil Nadu States.

## Three-keeled Mountain Lizard *Japalura tricarinata* 5cm

An open-forest living, ground-dwelling lizard from the Eastern Himalayas, with 6–8 conical scales on each side of the back of the head. Body small, not compressed; dorsal and nuchal crests absent; body and head with enlarged tuberculate scales; tail rounded; tympanum exposed; preanal and femoral pores absent; dorsum bright green, unpatterned or with dark brown, inverted V-shaped marks; lips with yellow or white spots; belly yellow or cream, sometimes with black spots. Inhabits open, rocky, forested hills. Diurnal and active on the ground, where it is associated with large rocks. Diet comprises insects. Reproductive habits unknown. Restricted to Sikkim and northern West Bengal States, in addition to Nepal.

## Variegated Mountain Lizard *Japalura variegata* 11cm

An eastern Himalayan lizard with hidden tympanum. Body somewhat compressed; limbs rather long; nuchal crest of elongated spines in males set on a skin fold; gular sac present; preanal and femoral pores absent; throat fold absent; dorsum bright green, with red, brown and green markings; back with light chevrons; forehead with light and dark cross-bars; belly greenish cream. Inhabits forested hills at elevations up to 2,700m. Diurnal and terrestrial. Diet comprises insects. Two clutches, each with 9–14 eggs are laid in a self-excavated hole in the soil, in May, June, September and November. Eggs are 6–7 × 10–12mm and incubation period is 50 days. Restricted to Sikkim and northern West Bengal, and also Nepal.

## Caucasian Agama *Laudakia caucasia* 15cm

A rock-dwelling species of lizard from the high Himalayas. A large, robust lizard; throat scales smooth; patch of enlarged scales on the middle of the sides; tail with distinct segmentation, each composed of double whorls of scales; dorsum olive to dark brown, and even yellow-ochre; head and tail usually lighter; back with numerous dark-edged orange ocelli, that become indistinct towards the back; throat of males spotted with bright yellow; belly unpatterned dark grey. Inhabits rocky outcrops, including cliffs, as well as boulders along river banks. Diurnal, basking on hot rocks during the midday sun. Diet comprises lizards and insects. About 12 eggs are laid between May and June. Besides Jammu and Kashmir State in northern India, this species occurs from Turkey, through Central Asia, to Iran and Pakistan.

## Himalayan Agama *Laudakia himalayana* 10cm

A rock-dwelling lizard from the Himalayas. A large, robust species; throat scales smooth; no patch of enlarged scales on sides of body; tail with distinct segmentation, each composed of double whorls of scales; dorsum dark olive-brown or bluish grey, with a light, vertebral stripe; scattered light spots on neck and shoulder; throat of males, and sometimes also the chest, marked with dark blue; belly greenish cream. Diurnal, found basking on rocky substrate, and feeds on insects. Hibernates during winter. Known from Jammu and Kashmir State, in addition to Pakistan, Nepal, Afghanistan, Turkemenistan and Tibet.

## Kashmiri Rock Agama *Laudakia tuberculata* 14cm

Yet another rock-dwelling species from the middle and upper ranges of the Himalayas. A large, robust lizard; throat scales keeled; patch of enlarged scales on middle of the sides; tail with distinct segmentation, each composed of double whorls of scales; dorsum dark olive-brown, dark-spotted in juveniles, spots broken up and modified into a speckled pattern of dark brown and yellow; chest, shoulder and sides with orange or yellow spots; belly brown or cream. Inhabits rock crevices, in colonies or singly. Males outnumber females. Breeding males develop a bright blue coloration when they bob their heads and produce a chirping sound. Mating takes place in March and August. Eggs are laid between April and October, clutches being 6–13, eggs measuring 20–22 × 11–12mm. A 31-day incubation period is known. Hibernation takes place between mid-October and the end of February. Insects, spiders, millipedes, centipedes, butterflies and flower petals are consumed. Widespread in the Western Himalayas, from the states of Jammu and Kashmir to Himachal Pradesh and Uttar Pradesh, and also, Nepal, Pakistan and Afghanistan.

## Indian Kangaroo Lizard *Otocryptis beddomii* 5cm

A forest-dwelling lizard that runs on its hindlimbs when threatened, which is confined to the Western Ghats. Body compressed; dorsal scales keeled; dorsal crest absent; tympanum not visible; dorsum light brown, the vertebral region paler than the sides; sometimes a series of brown, transverse spots are present; forehead with a dark bar. Inhabits moist deciduous and evergreen forests, in leaf litter, and rarely, in low vegetation, such as shrubs and tree trunks. Clutches comprise 3–5 eggs. Restricted to the southern part of the Ghats, in Kerala and south-western Tamil Nadu States.

## Theobald's Toad-headed Agama *Phrynocephalus theobaldi*
5cm

This agama inhabits high and extremely arid regions, such as Ladakh, to the west of the Tibetan Plateau, with sand and stones as substrate, and treeless. Body depressed; lacking a dorsal crest or gular sac; head rather large; limbs small; dorsum grey, speckled with black, white and brown; usually a series of paired black spots along the back or 2 dorso-lateral stripes; tail rounded, its tip blunt. Inhabits arid, sandy regions at altitudes up to 5,100m and lives in colonies. Burrows are up to 25cm into the ground, concealed by stones or tufts of grass. This is a terrestrial and pugnacious species when threatened, gaping and keeping the body off the ground. Ants, beetles, grasshoppers and spiders are consumed. These lizards may be oviparous or viviparous, and monogamous, clutch size is 2, between June and August. Known from Jammu and Kashmir State, and also Nepal, Tibet and Turkestan.

## South Indian Rock Agama *Psammophilus dorsalis* 14cm

Another large-headed, pugnacious, rock-dwelling lizard from the Indian Peninsula. Body robust, flattened; no dorsal crest; scales uniform, keeled; a deep fold in front of shoulder; 115–150 scales around the middle of the body; dorsum of adult males brown, a dark brown or black stripe along the side of the body; belly yellow. Juveniles and adult females olive-brown, with dark brown spots and speckles and elongated white spots on sides of neck. During the breeding season, the upper parts of the body of adult males become bright red or orange; the undersurfaces a contrasting intense black. Diurnal and active in rocky regions, where they feed on insects. Clutch size is 7–8, eggs measuring 6 × 12mm, produced between May and June. More than one clutch is laid per season. Widespread from Bihar State, down through the Eastern Ghats, to the low hills of the Western Ghats.

## Green Fan-throated Lizard *Ptyctolaemus gularis* 8cm

A fan-throated lizard from north-eastern India, frequently seen basking on walls in towns as well as in forests. Head long and slender; body compressed; dorsal scales keeled; dorsal crest absent; 3 longitudinal folds on each side of throat that curve to meet on the back; a gular sac that extends when excited; dorsum olive-brown, fold on back deep blue; 5 broad transverse bands on body; a green dorso-lateral band on sides of front of body; sides with a network of dark brown, that enclose rounded areas of green. Inhabits montane forests, as well as urban habitats. Arboreal and diurnal, activities span the end of March to early November. Diet comprises insects, spiders and soil arthropods. Nests are produced in mid-May, when 14–15 spherical eggs, of 7–12mm are produced. Hatchlings emerge around the end of August. Restricted to Meghalaya, Mizoram, Arunachal Pradesh and Nagaland States in north-eastern India, as well as adjacent regions of Tibet.

## Anaimalai Spiny Lizard *Salea anamalayana* 20cm

A slow-moving, montane lizard from the Western Ghats. Head large; dorsal crest distinct, continuous with the nuchal crest; body compressed; a strong fold in front of the shoulder; dorsal scales unequal; dorsum with V-shaped dark brown marks, separated by narrow cream-coloured areas; head brown, white-spotted; lips white, the colour extending to the shoulder; belly white. A diurnal, arboreal species that feeds on insects. Up to 3 clutches may be produced in a season (in April), each comprising 3–5 eggs, measuring 7 × 16mm. Known only from the Anaimalai and Palni Hills of western Tamil Nadu State.

## Horsfield's Spiny Lizard *Salea horsfieldii* 25cm

Another montane lizard from the Western Ghats. Head large, dorsal crest distinct, continuous with the nuchal crest; no fold in front of the shoulder; body compressed; dorsal scales equal; dorsum green or greyish cream, with dark grey or dark brown cross-bars or irregular blotches on the back and sides; a dark band, edged with white runs from eye to shoulder; belly cream, spotted with brown. Diurnal, arboreal lizard that is insectivorous. Clutch size is 3–4, and egg-laying may continue until at least September. Restricted to the Nilgiri and Palni Hills of western Tamil Nadu State.

## Fan-throated Lizard *Sitana ponticeriana* 8cm

A fast, bipedal lizard from open areas that is capable of running on its hindlimbs, with its tail raised. Snout rather acute; tympanum present; hindlimbs elongated, with only 4 toes; scales keeled; femoral pores absent; tail long and slender; dewlap large, projecting in males; gular fold absent; dorsum brown, with dark brown, black-edged, diamond-shaped marks; mouth-lining dark blue; dewlap blue on the tip, dark blue in the middle and red at the base; belly cream. This lizard is found in scrub forests, sea beaches and the edges of arid regions. Diurnal and terrestrial, its diet comprises termites, beetles and bugs. Eggs are produced in October, 6–8 at a time, measuring 6 × 10mm. Widespread in northern and Peninsular India, besides Nepal, Pakistan and Sri Lanka.

# CHAMAELEONIDAE (CHAMAELEONS)

The sole representative of an otherwise essentially Afro-Madagascan family, our single species occurs in the drier regions of southern Asia. A few enter the Middle East and southern Europe. They feed primarily on insects that are caught with the help of their exceedingly long and sticky tongues. Most species are arboreal, and all are active during the day. Unusual among lizards are the eyes, which are capable of moving independently of each other, and the opposable fingers and toes. The tails of chamaeleons are highly prehensile and effectively function as a fifth limb, assisting in climbing and hanging from branches of trees.

**South Asian Chamaeleon** *Chamaeleo zeylanicus* 18cm

(Top) *Full body;*
(above) *close-up of head*

A single species of these amazing lizards is found in India, as opposed to several dozen species in Madagascar and Africa, where these lizards have undergone radiation. Head with a distinct helmet-like bony projection; orbit of eye large; eyeball covered with skin, leaving a tiny aperture; scales on body enlarged, tuberculate; a low, serrated dorsal crest extending to prehensile tail; fingers and toes opposable. Males show a spur-like projection on hindlimbs. Arboreal, inhabiting shrubs and trees. These lizards have a remarkable capacity to change body colour, from green to yellow, with spots or bands. Diet comprises insects, to capture which its tongue can be extended for nearly the length of the body. Eggs number 10–31 in a clutch, each 10–13 × 16–19mm, and are leathery-textured. In Gujarat State, western India, eggs are produced in early winter (November). Widespread in the arid and semi-arid regions of western and Peninsular India; also, northern Sri Lanka and extreme eastern Pakistan.

# DIBAMIDAE (WORM LIZARDS)

Worm lizards are perhaps the least well known of all living families of lizards, and are distributed on the mainland and the islands of south-east Asia, up to New Guinea. All live under the soil or in rotting logs, presumably where their main food – termites and earthworms – are plentiful. They are only occasionally unearthed, and are not frequently collected, perhaps on account of their superficial similarity to earthworms, and due to their secretive habits. The eggs of dibamids are longer than broad, brittle, with a highly calcareous shell similar to that of geckos, and may be laid under bark at the base of rotting tree trunks or under the soil.

**Nicobarese Worm Lizard** *Dibamus nicobaricum* 13cm

A limbless lizard known only from some of the islands of the Nicobars. Snout conical; head covered with enlarged scales; body long; head distinct from neck; fore and hindlimbs absent in females; in males, hindlimbs in the form of flaps on each side of the vent; tail short; dorsal scales smooth; dorsum iridescent chestnut, with a light cream neck and throat band; a darker cream mid-body band that grades into chestnut at the back; belly flesh-coloured; a pale spot over vent. Little is known of the natural history of this burrowing species. One was found in alluvial soil, under a stone, within a primary rainforest. Others were collected under debris inside a forest. Its diet is unknown, however, it is likely to comprise soft-bodied invertebrates, such as insect pupae and earthworms. It is known only from Kamorta and Great Nicobar Island, in the Bay of Bengal.

# EUBLEPHARIDAE (LEOPARD GECKOS)

These geckos differ from typical geckos in showing fleshy eyelids. Their distribution includes both the New and the Old Worlds. Most species (except the south-east Asian ones that are forest dwellers) inhabit scrub forests and deserts. All feed on invertebrates.

## Western Indian Leopard Gecko *Eublepharis fuscus* 25cm

A stout lizard, with a large head, snout bluntly pointed; distinct fleshy eyelids; enlarged smooth tubercles on dorsum; deep axillary pockets; femoral pores absent; digits slender; lamellae under toes entire, smooth; subcaudals enlarged; dorsum of adults light brown or drab, with a single, broad band between the nuchal loop and caudal constriction; darker variegations within the pale bands on body and neck; juveniles with alternate pale–dark bands on dorsum; belly dull brown or grey. Crepuscular, insectivorous, terrestrial and inhabits dry forests, scrub and rocky biotope. Restricted to the plains on the west coast of India, from southern Gujarat to Maharashtra and possibly central Karnataka State.

## Common Asian Leopard Gecko *Eublepharis macularius* 16cm

A familiar leopard gecko from the western parts of the Subcontinent. Body stout; conical dorsal tubercles; dorsum of adults, pale yellow to brownish yellow; with small, blue-black spots that may form reticulations; juveniles dark brown to black dorsally, with 2–3 yellow bands across trunk, in addition to a white nuchal loop; tail with 4–6 bands. These lizards conceal themselves in rocky crevices, under rock piles or in small mammal burrows, in rocky deserts as well as scrub forests. Nocturnal, terrestrial and social, they are found in colonies. Hibernates between November to early March. Crickets, grasshoppers, beetles, dragonflies, antlions, scorpions and other lizards are eaten. Clutches of 1–2 (sometimes 3) eggs, 13–16 × 31–35mm, are laid between March and June, with several clutches produced in a year. Hatchlings emerge between September and October. Known from Rajasthan as well as Jammu, besides Pakistan, Afghanistan and, possibly, Iran.

# GEKKONIDAE (GECKOS)

Geckos are familiar to all city dwellers – this family includes species commonly found in human dwellings. House geckos actually include several species, and many are commensals of humans. However, most species of geckos are found in undisturbed habitats, from forests to scrubland and even on desert dunes. All species are primarily insectivorous, tending to sit in wait for insects of an appropriate size to come within striking distance. Their tails are detachable, a new one replacing the one lost.

## Indian Golden Gecko *Calodactylodes aureus* 9cm

A large, brightly coloured, rock-dwelling gecko that lives communally in rocky outcrops of Peninsular India. The head is rather large; the body covered with small flat scales, with scattered rounded tubercles; undersurface of the fingers and toes with plate-like expanded scansors; adult males with 2 preanal pores; 1–6 femoral pores.

(Top) *Hatchlings*, (above) *adult*

Adult males, especially the dominant one in the colony, are bright yellow, particularly on the throat. Others are olive-yellow, reddish brown or blackish brown. Its distinctive calls, comprising a series of four notes, is heard at dusk. Scansors at the tip are wedge-shaped, supposedly adaptive for clinging on to rocky surfaces. Diet comprises grasshoppers, beetles, butterflies and their larvae, spiders, ants and lizard eggs. Clutches of 2 eggs are produced in January in communal nests that are on rock faces and clefts, and have even been reported from the walls of a fort. Eggs measure 12–13 × 14–15mm and hatchlings measure 2.8–2.9cm. Recorded from Andhra Pradesh and northern Tamil Nadu States, of south-eastern India.

**Assamese Day Gecko** *Cnemaspis assamensis* 3cm

A tiny, tree-trunk dwelling species of gecko from north-eastern India. Head distinct from neck; eyes large, with rounded pupils; ventral scales increase in size from chin to throat; spines on sides of body absent; tubercles on dorsum of body absent; smooth scales on belly; preanal and femoral pores absent; 2–5 enlarged scansors of toes; tail segmented, with flattened scales forming whorls; dorsum light brown, with a buff, vertebral stripe, a chevron-like pale pattern on back, dark-edged posteriorly; a cream, transverse bar at back of head; a black, nuchal spot; belly unpatterned, cream. Inhabits subtropical evergreen forests, where they are active during the day on low tree trunks. Diet is presumably insects. Two spherical eggs are produced in June. Known only from Kamrup District, western Assam, in north-eastern India.

**Indian Day Gecko** *Cnemaspis indica* 4cm

Another small, day-active gecko from the southern ranges of the Western Ghats. Head distinct from neck; snout elongate; eyes large, with rounded pupils; dorsal scales keeled; spines on sides of body absent; tubercles on dorsum of body absent; smooth scales on belly; 4–5 femoral pores; tail segmented, with flattened scales forming whorls; dorsum light brown, with red or orange spots and mottlings; belly brownish cream; throat dark brown. Diurnal, and active on tree trunks and rocks; insectivorous. A hatchling was obtained from an egg measuring $7 \times 8$mm in March. It was found in a tree buttress, half buried in loose soil. Known from the Nilgiri Hills and Travancore region of western Tamil Nadu and Kerala States.

## Coastal Day Gecko *Cnemaspis littoralis* 3cm

Another small, day-active gecko from the southern ranges of the Western Ghats. Head distinct from neck; snout elongate; eyes large, with rounded pupils; body slender; dorsal granular; conical spines on sides of body; tubercles on dorsum of body; ventral scales smooth; 14–18 femoral pores; tail segmented, with flattened scales forming whorls; 3–5 very large scansors under toes; dorsum greyish brown, with dark-edged, grey spots on the vertebral region; a dark stripe along the side of head, and one between the lower lip and the ear; belly greyish cream. Diurnal, and active on tree trunks in evergreen and deciduous forests. Insectivorous, its reproductive habits are unknown. Restricted to the western slopes of the Nilgiri and Ponmudi Hills, in western Tamil Nadu and Kerala States.

## Ponmudi Day Gecko *Cnemaspis nairi* 4cm

A small, forest-dwelling species of day gecko from the southern Western Ghats. Snout long, pointed; ventral scales smooth; sides of body lacking spinous projections; males with 7–8 preanal pores, but no femoral pores; dorsum olive-grey, with pairs of paravertebral, black spots, each followed by a white, vertebral spot; scales on sides cream; tail with black and olive-yellow rings; belly greyish brown. Diurnal, it hides under rocks and fallen logs and is generally distributed in evergreen and semi-evergreen forests of Kerala, in the southern Western Ghats, at altitudes of 280–925m.

## Ota's Day Gecko *Cnemaspis otai* 3cm

A small, rock-dwelling species of gecko, this is the only representative of its genus on the Eastern Ghats. Head large; snout longer than eye; eye large with rounded pupil; body slender, elongate; dorsal tubercles scattered; no spine-like tubercles on flanks; three preanal pores; four femoral pores; dorsum greyish brown, with three pairs of black paravertebral spots that are partially fused on the vertebral region; belly yellowish cream. Diurnal and rock-dwelling, it is also found in abandoned wells. Of its diet and reproduction, nothing is on record. Known only from Vellore Fort and adjacent hillocks, in Andhra Pradesh, south-eastern India.

## Rough-bellied Day Gecko *Cnemaspis tropidogaster* 4cm

A relatively uncommon, day-active lizard from the hills of the southern Western Ghats. Head distinct from body; snout elongated; spinous tubercles on sides of body; ventral scales keeled; males with 2–4 preanal and 3–6 femoral pores; dorsum dark brown, with lighter and darker variegations arranged transversely; spinous tubercles on sides of body cream; belly pale brown. Diurnal, active in rocky substrates and low trunks of trees, and occasionally entering man-made structures, such as thatched huts and cow-sheds. Known from the Western Ghats and from the central highlands of Sri Lanka.

## Flat-tailed Gecko *Cosymbotus platyurus* 7cm

A fringe of skin on sides of body and back of hindlimbs identify this house gecko. Snout rather long; fingers and toes almost half-webbed; body depressed, smooth, with tiny granules; 7–9 lamellae under fourth toe; males with 34–36 femoral pores; dorsum light grey, sometimes with darker variegations, usually with a dark grey streak between eye and shoulder; belly unpatterned cream. Large numbers may take up residence inside a house, although only one or two will inhabit a single room, larger animals actively chasing away smaller intruders. During the day, they hide behind book shelves and in cracks in woodwork, emerging at dusk to wait in ambush for insects, usually close to electric light-bulbs. Nesting is sometimes communal, eggs laid in retreat sites. Eggs measure 9 × 10–11mm and hatchlings are 2.1–2.5cm. Found in eastern and north-eastern India and the Andaman and Nicobar Islands, and also Nepal and Bangladesh, east to eastern China and south-east Asia.

## Sindh Sand Gecko *Crossobamon orientalis* 5cm

Shomen Mukherjee

A small, dainty desert gecko. Head rather large; dorsal scales small, mixed with rounded tubercles, ventral scales small, smooth; fingers and toes with a fringe of small, pointed scales; femoral pores sometimes absent in males, when present may number 1–4; dorsum brownish yellow to pale grey, with 3–5 indistinct grey bands; tail yellow with distinct dark rings; belly cream. Inhabits sand dunes and areas with fine sand and sparse vegetation. Terrestrial and nocturnal, they burrow into the sand, and are most active between March and early April, and also October–November. When threatened, they emit a low, snarling sound, and produce excrement. Termites and other insects are consumed. Clutches comprise 3 eggs that are produced between March and April. Restricted to western India (Rajasthan State's Thar Desert), and the adjacent region of Pakistan (Sindh Province).

## Nicobar Bent-toed Gecko *Cyrtodactylus adleri* 7cm

A brightly coloured, forest gecko from the rainforests of the Nicobar Islands. Head long; snout tapering; ear-opening small, oval; digits slender, recurved, not dilated, with enlarged lamellae on the ventral surface; tail with tubercles, long, tapering to a fine point; 2 enlarged tubercles on each side of the vent; six preanal pores in males; preanal groove absent; dorsum and forehead brown, the latter with 7 dark rounded blotches; a dark line from posterior corner of eyes to armpit; and two dark spots on the neck region; tail with 10 dark bands. Inhabits lowland rainforests and is arboreal and nocturnal. There is no information on its diet or reproduction. When threatened, they raise and curl their tails, like many other members of this group of geckos. Restricted to Great Nicobar Island in the Bay of Bengal.

## Khasi Hills Bent-toed Gecko *Cyrtodactylus khasiensis* 9cm

A common, rock-dwelling gecko from the Eastern Himalayas. Snout relatively long; dorsal surface of body and limbs with small, granular scales, intermixed with larger, keeled tubercles; a lateral fold of enlarged scales; males with 12–14 preanal pores; femoral pores absent; dorsum dark greyish brown, with dark spots; a dark curved mark extends across the nape to join the eyes; forehead black-spotted; belly cream. Nocturnal, active on rocks and low vegetation, in the foothills and low hills. During the day, it shelters inside rotten tree trunks. Diet comprises insects. Reproductive habits are unknown. Fairly widespread in north-eastern India, including northern West Bengal, Assam, Meghalaya and Arunachal Pradesh, this species is also known from Bhutan and northern Myanmar.

## Lawder's Bent-toed Gecko *Cyrtodactylus lawderanus* 6cm

A common, rock-dwelling gecko from the Western Himalayas. Snout relatively short; dorsal surface of body and limbs with small, granular scales, with only a few tubercles; an indistinct lateral skin fold sometimes present; males with an angular series of 4–5 preanal pores; femoral pores absent; tail cylindrical, swollen at base; dorsum greyish brown, with wavy, dark brown cross-bars; belly greyish cream. Nocturnal and found on rocks and low vegetation. Diet comprises insects. Reproductive habits unknown. Recorded from the mid-hills of Himachal Pradesh and Uttar Pradesh.

## Andaman Bent-toed Gecko *Cyrtodactylus rubidus* 8cm

A brightly coloured, forest gecko from the rainforests of the Andaman Islands. Head long; snout tapering; ear-opening small, oval, digits with enlarged lamellae on the ventral surface; tail with tubercles, long, tapering to a fine point; 3 enlarged tubercles on each side of the vent; 6 preanal pores in males; preanal groove present; dorsum and forehead reddish brown to dark grey-black, the latter with a series of transverse bands, typically complete, but occasionally connected medially to form a network of reticulations; a dark line from posterior corner of eyes to armpit; tail with 10 dark bands. Inhabits lowland rainforests, sometimes entering human habitation, and is arboreal and nocturnal. Diet comprises small insects, and 2 oval eggs are produced at a time. When threatened, they raise and curl their tails, like many bent-toed geckos. Restricted to Andaman Islands in the Bay of Bengal.

**Warty Rock Gecko** *Cyrtopodion kachhense*  4cm

A rock-dwelling, warty gecko from the dry western part of the country. Head fairly large; snout blunt; eyes large, with vertical pupils; head scales small, with larger tubercles; body flattened; fingers and toes slender; dorsal tubercles small, smaller than those on the sides, in longitudinal series that are separated by 3–5 rows of smaller granules; blunt spines on tail, comprising lateral rows of scales; males with 4–7 preanal pores; dorsum light brown or grey, with small, irregularly arranged dark spots; belly cream. Nocturnal, it is found in rocky areas, and often found in buildings. They are abundant especially after heavy showers. Diet unknown, and presumably comprises small insects. Clutches include 1–2 eggs, measuring $7 \times 10$mm that may be produced almost throughout the year. Indian records are only from western Rajasthan and Gujarat States, in western India, the range of the species includes Pakistan and probably also Iran.

**Keeled Rock Gecko** *Cyrtopodion scabrum*  6cm

A medium-sized, dry-region gecko, entering India in the west. Head fairly large; snout blunt; eyes large, with vertical pupils; head scales small, with larger tubercles; body flattened; fingers and toes slender; dorsal tubercles large, in longitudinal series that are separated by one or two rows of smaller granules; blunt spines on tail, comprising lateral rows of scales; mid-ventrals enlarged; males with 4–7 preanal pores; dorsum light grey to tan, with irregularly arranged dark spots forming cross-bands on tail; belly cream. Nocturnal, it is found in dry grasslands, sandy deserts and rocky terrain, often in the vicinity of human habitation. Insects, such as ants, beetles and flies are consumed. Two eggs, measuring $7 \times 10$mm are produced between March and August. Found in the western-most portion of Rajasthan State in western India, the range of the species extending from Egypt and Ethiopia, through the Middle East, to southern Asia. Introduced via human agencies to North America.

**Kollegal Ground Gecko** *Geckoella collegalensis* 5cm

A dainty, colourful, ground-dwelling gecko from the plains of western Peninsular India. Body stout, cylindrical, covered with small, granular scales; scales on belly overlapping; tail short, tapering, regenerated tail turnip-shaped; dorsum with 5 pairs of large dark brown spots, in addition to 3 pairs on head; tail with 11 dark brown bands. Inhabits deciduous and scrub forests that may border wetlands. Crepuscular, hiding under rocks during the day and emerging at dusk to forage for insects, such as termites. Clutches comprise 2 eggs, measuring 9 × 10–11mm that are produced in August, and hatch in October. Incubation period is 43 days. Hatchlings measure 3.4cm in total length. Widely distributed from Gir forest in southern Gujarat State, south through Maharashtra, Karnataka, Kerala and Tamil Nadu States, from the foothills of the Western Ghats.

**Deccan Ground Gecko** *Geckoella dekkanensis* 8cm

Vivek Gur-Broom

A white-banded, ground-dwelling gecko from the low country of the northern Western Ghats. Body stout, cylindrical, covered with small, granular scales; head moderately large; scales on belly overlapping; tail short, weakly swollen at base and tapering; males lack pores, but have enlarged preanal and femoral scales; dorsum reddish brown, with narrow, dark-edged, white, transverse bands; tail also with white bands; belly unpatterned cream. Inhabits dry, flat scrub and thinly forested areas. Nothing is known of its diet or reproductive habits. Restricted to Maharashtra State.

**Clouded Ground Gecko** *Geckoella nebulosa*  5cm

A pretty, terrestrial gecko from the broken hills of the east coast and the central plateau of India. Body stout, cylindrical, covered with enlarged tubercles; head moderately large; scales on belly overlapping; tail short, swollen at base and tapering; males lack preanal and femoral pores or enlarged scales on preanal or thigh regions; dorsum light brown or greyish brown, with a pair of dark brown, rounded, sinuous spots that continue to the tail; belly unpatterned light brown. Inhabits scrub and other types of open forests. Terrestrial and insectivorous, hiding under stones during the day. Its reproductive habits are unknown. Distributed from Puri and Koraput District of Orissa State, to Gorge, Golconda and other isolated hills in Andhra Pradesh.

**Four-clawed Gecko** *Gehyra mutilata*  6cm

A beautiful house gecko, recognized by the absence of a claw on the inner digit. Head relatively large, skin delicate and tail flattened, widening at base, with sharp, somewhat denticulate edges; large, flat scales on tail and belly; males with 25–41 preano-femoral pores; dorsum pale almost translucent grey to pinkish grey, usually with a pale vertebral area; an indistinct white band along the face; belly pale pink. Found in both human habitation and primary forests. Nocturnal, its diet comprises insects. Two eggs are produced at a time, measuring 8 × 11mm, that are fused together, in February and July. Hatchlings measure 1.7–2.3cm. Range includes isolated localities in northern and southern India, including Uttar Pradesh and Kerala States, as well as Sri Lanka, east to Myanmar, Indo-China, the Malay Peninsula and Archipelago, to Oceania. This species seem to have increased its range recently through human activities, being easily transported by man with timber.

## Tokay Gecko *Gekko gecko* 18cm

A very large, brightly coloured, noisy house gecko from eastern India, it is also found in undisturbed forest. Head large; body thick-set, with granular scales; males with 13–24 preanal pores; dorsum slaty grey, with red or orange spots; tail dark-banded; belly cream, unpatterned or variegated with grey; eye yellow. The loud call of this gecko gives the species, as well as the genus, their names. Calls may be uttered under distress, but more commonly heard are territorial calls, produced with the aid of well-developed vocal cords. Clutches comprise 2 spherical eggs, measuring 25mm, that are laid in tree-holes. Incubation period is 64 days and hatchlings measure 4.0–4.2cm. This species is known from Bihar, West Bengal, Assam and Tripura States, besides Nepal, Bangladesh, the range of the species including southern China and mainland and insular south-east Asia, up to Sulawesi and the Philippines.

## Smith's Giant Gecko *Gekko smithii* 19cm

Smith's Giant Gecko is another loud gecko. Head large; body thick-set, with scattered tubercles on dorsum; males with 11–16 preanal pores in a short angular series; dorsum greyish brown, with a transverse series of white spots, tail dark-banded; belly cream, with grey patches; eye green. The call of this gecko is reminiscent of the bark of a dog, commonly heard at night from forested habitats, although it is known to enter houses on occasion. Diet comprises insects and 2 eggs are laid at a time, glued on to tree trunks. This gecko is known from the Nicobar Islands of India, and also Thailand, Peninsular Malaysia, Sumatra, Java and Borneo.

### Anaimalai Gecko *Hemidactylus anamallensis* 4.5cm

A rock-dwelling gecko with undivided toe scansors from the mid-hills of the Western Ghats. Head depressed; snout pointed; forehead and back covered with small granular scales; belly with large overlapping scales; weak webs on toes; tail covered with small scales; males with 40–44 preano-femoral pores; dorsum greyish brown, spotted or marbled with dark brown; belly pale brown. Nocturnal, inhabiting open forested areas with loose boulders, occasionally entering human habitation. It is insectivorous and produces 1–2 eggs, measuring 7–8 × 9–10mm, between December and June, that hatch after 63–68 days. Hatchlings are 1.8–2.1cm in snout–vent length. Known from the Western Ghats at Anaimalai, Palni, Tirunelveli and Eravikulam. In some works, this gecko is placed in the genus *Dravidogecko* on account of the undivided scansors of toes.

### Bowring's Gecko *Hemidactylus bowringii* 5cm

A rather nondescript house gecko from eastern India. Head relatively large; snout pointed; males with 12–15 femoral pores; tail base not swollen, without denticulate edges; dorsum light brown, with darker spots; a dark streak along the side of the head; sometimes, 4 longitudinal streaks along back; tail with dark chevrons; belly unpatterned cream. Inhabits human-modified habitats and enters houses. Nocturnal and insectivorous, laying 2 eggs at a time. Isolated records from eastern India, including Andhra Pradesh, Sikkim, northern West Bengal, besides Bangladesh, east to Myanmar and eastern China.

## Brooke's House Gecko *Hemidactylus brookii* 6cm

A common, rough-skinned gecko from northern India. Head oval; head scales small; body flattened; with granular scales and rows of tubercles; tail plump with spine-like tubercles on dorsum; dorsum dark brown to light grey, with dark spots usually arranged in groups; belly cream. Inhabits parks, gardens and houses, as well as open forests. Largely terrestrial, although sometimes found climbing low walls, from deserts, thinly wooded country to human habitation. Nocturnal, it is active during the hot and wet months, hibernating during the winter. Its loud 'chuck-chuck-chuck' call is commonly heard after dark. Diet comprises small insects. Two eggs are produced between March and October, measuring 7 × 9mm, and more than a single clutch may be laid. Eggs hatch in approximately 43 days. Distributed over northern India; also, Pakistan, and introduced populations have been found on Borneo, West Africa, southern China and the West Indies.

## Yellow-green House Gecko *Hemidactylus flaviviridis* 7cm

Another common house gecko from northern India, this is a smooth-textured, large-growing species, scuttling behind pelmets and photo frames at the first sign of danger. Head oval; head scales small; body flattened; dorsum lacking tubercles; tail sometimes with two pairs of rows of tubercles; males with fewer than 15 preano-femoral pores; dorsum pale grey at night to olive by day, when they may show dark cross-bars; belly light yellow. Arboreal and found as a human commensal. Diet comprises flies, bugs, mole crickets, beetles, termites, spiders and moths. Mating takes place between February and November, although egg-laying has been observed in the months of January, March, April and June, and therefore, some populations probably breed throughout the year. Usually 2, sometimes 3, oval, elliptical, hard-shelled eggs are produced at a time, laid in crevices on walls or behind book cases. Eggs hatch between August and September, incubation period being 33–68 days and hatchlings measuring 1.1cm. Widespread in northern and eastern India. This species is known from the shores of the Red Sea in northern Africa and the Middle East to southern Asia.

## Asian House Gecko *Hemidactylus frenatus* 7cm

A small but loud house gecko, widespread in Peninsular India. Head large, dorsal scales smooth; lack of webbing in fingers and toes; skin; sides of tail showing enlarged tubercles; no flaps of skin along sides of body and at back of hindlimbs; males showing 28–36 preano-femoral pores; dorsum greyish brown, sometimes with darker markings; a brown streak, with a light edge on top, runs along the side of the head, sometimes continuing along the side of the body; belly unpatterned cream. Its call is a series of 4–5 loud, staccato notes. Insects and spiders form the mainstay of its diet. Inhabits man-made structures, as well as forested areas. Two eggs, measuring 8 × 10mm, are produced. Widespread in southern India, and introduced into almost every part of the tropics and subtropics by human activities.

## Garnot's Gecko *Hemidactylus garnoti* 7cm

A parthenogenetic species, producing eggs without mating and no males have ever been found. Head large; dorsal scales small; tail depressed, with denticulate lateral edges; 14–19 enlarged femoral scales; dorsum brownish grey, sometimes with brown and cream spots; belly unpatterned cream. Inhabits trees as well as the walls of buildings, frequently entering houses. A parthenogenetic species, producing 2 eggs at a time. Known from eastern India, including Sikkim, northern West Bengal and Assam States, as well as Bhutan, mainland south-east Asia and the islands of the Pacific Ocean.

**Bark Gecko** *Hemidactylus leschenaultii* 8cm

A large-growing, smooth-textured house gecko from Peninsular and western India. Head large; body robust; tail depressed, its lateral edge spinose; scales small; males with 12–19 femoral pores; dorsum pale grey, with dark grey or black, wavy cross-bars or a series of W-shaped patterns, coloration darker in juveniles; belly unpatterned cream or grey. It inhabits lightly wooded country, and is often seen on large trees. Frequently, it enters houses and feeds on insects, and is also a known predator of the Asian House Gecko. Clutches comprise 2 eggs, laid in March. Widespread from West Bengal, south to Tamil Nadu, and also the dry northern parts of Sri Lanka and eastern Pakistan.

**Spotted Rock Gecko** *Hemidactylus maculatus* 28cm

A large rock gecko from the low hills of Peninsular India. Snout pointed; forehead with large scattered scales; ventrals smooth; dorsum greyish brown, with black blotches that may be fused to form wavy bars; belly unpatterned cream. Inhabits rocky outcrops, including caves and cracks in boulders, and more rarely on walls of buildings and on trees. Diet comprises insects and other geckos. Two eggs are laid communally on rock surfaces, 9–10 × 11–12mm in March and August; hatchlings 3.1cm. Restricted to the foothills of the Western Ghats, from southern Dangs, Gujarat, up to the Tirunelveli and Shevaroy Hills of Tamil Nadu, and also Sri Lanka.

99

**Reticulated Gecko** *Hemidactylus reticulatus* 4cm

A dainty, terrestrial gecko that hides under stones in the scrub forests of the southern Deccan. Head relatively short; snout rounded; forehead covered with small granular scales; back with small keeled scales, intermixed with larger, pointed tubercles; tail rounded and covered with pointed tubercles; males with 6–12 preanal pores; dorsum brown, with a network of darker lines forming a reticulate pattern; belly cream; throat sometimes with brown streaks. Inhabits open forests, such as scrubland. Nocturnal, it hides during the day under rocks and stones. Diet and reproductive habits unknown. Known from Karnataka and Tamil Nadu States.

**Termite-hill Gecko** *Hemidactylus triedrus* 8cm

A beautiful, banded gecko. Head large; an indistinct lateral skin fold present; dorsum with 16–18 rows of large, convex tubercles; dorsum yellowish olive, with 3 large, brown, saddle-like patches, edged with black; head with yellow stripes from behind eye and across nape; belly unpatterned cream. Inhabits open forests and scrubland. Nocturnal and terrestrial, it shelters during the day in rock cracks and rodent burrows. Diet comprises termites, and also crickets, grasshoppers, spiders and beetles, and known to congregate on termitaria with swarming termite alates. Clutches comprise 2, reportedly even 6, eggs, 10 × 11–12mm, laid between May and July. Hatchlings 2.2cm. Also known from Sri Lanka and eastern Pakistan.

**Western Ghats Worm Gecko** *Hemiphyllodactylus aurantiacus* 3.5cm

A rather elongated, short-legged gecko from southern India. Head slightly distinct from neck; 9 preanal pores; 7–8 femoral pores in adult males; dorsum light to mid-brown; belly with an orange-red flush, with darker specklings, and can be differentiated from the closely-related Oceanic Worm Gecko in showing a bolder pattern on body, comprising two series of thin, black stripes, a dark stripe under eye and distinctly banded tail; a general reduction (2–3) in the number of scansors on toes (as opposed to 3–6) and is a bisexual species, both males and females being known. Found under stones in forested habitats and on walls of houses. Nocturnal, and active on relatively dark portion of walls, presumably to avoid competition with larger house geckos. Two spherical eggs, measuring 5mm are produced at a time, in January. Records are from the Shevaroy Hills, Anaimalai of Tamil Nadu and Bangalore, in Karnataka State.

**Oceanic Worm Gecko** *Hemiphyllodactylus typus* 6cm

A tiny gecko, with an elongated body and short-legs. Head slightly distinct from neck; granular dorsal scales; ventral scales smooth, rounded and imbricate; digits free; scansors divided, numbering 3–6; terminal phalange short, clawed; tail prehensile; males with 10–12 angular series of preanal pores, usually separated from 8–10 femoral pores; dorsum dark brown, with dark brown blotches; a dark brown stripe from nostril to shoulder, belly cream, with dark brown speckles. This nocturnal gecko is active on trees from coastal localities up to nearly 1,000 m, and may also be seen on the walls of houses, where it hunts small insects. A unisexual and parthenogenetic species, eggs, measuring 6 × 8mm, are laid in pairs in hollows of dead branches, inside rotting logs and the axils of ferns, in April, and produce hatchlings, 1.4–1.8cm. Common in mangroves and can also be a commensal of man. Recorded from the Andaman Islands of India, besides Sri Lanka, Thailand, the Malay Peninsula, Borneo, the Philippines, east to Oceania and Hawaii, although more than a single species is suspected to be called by this name.

## Mourning Gecko *Lepidodactylus lugubris* 4.2cm

A strange-looking, rather elongate, rarely seen gecko from mangroves. Head longer than broad; body elongated; tubercles on dorsum absent; preano-femoral scales 25–31; dorsum cinnamon brown or greyish brown, with brownish-red tail; a dark stripe along the face; cross-bars on body and tail W-shaped; belly cream. Found on leaves and branches of mangrove trees, especially at night, when they emerge to forage. Some populations are unisexual, parthenogenetic, producing fertile eggs without mating with males. Clutches include 2 eggs, laid on leaves, sometimes communally, measuring 7 × 10mm. Hatchlings are 17–18mm. In India, this species is restricted to the Andaman and Nicobar Islands, but it also occurs in Sri Lanka; its distribution encompasses almost the whole of south-east Asia, eastwards to the South-west Pacific, forming a constellation of cryptic species, some of which remain unnamed.

## Andaman Day Gecko *Phelsuma andamanense* 15cm

A bright green and red (especially in males) diurnal gecko, found abundantly on coconut trees and other vegetation, including the trunks and branches of large trees on the Andaman (but strangely, not on the Nicobar) Islands. A small gecko; claws reduced and sometimes absent; scales small, granular; eyelid present; pupil rounded; fingers and toes with rounded tips, with undivided scansors below; males with 15 preano-femoral pores. Adult males have bright red markings on a green dorsum and a bluish-green tail, females are unpatterned green; belly cream; throat yellow. Active during the day on trees as well as plantations of coconuts and bananas, occasionally entering areas of human habitation. Two oval eggs are produced, clutches deposited in sheltered locations, such as the undersurface of palm fronds; breeding occurring year round. Restricted to the Andaman Islands, in the Bay of Bengal. Other members of the genus are found in eastern Africa, Madagascar and the Seychelles.

# LACERTIDAE (LACERTAS)

Lacertas are primarily lizards of colder, open areas of Europe and central Asia, relatively few species making it to India, and the greatest diversity is to be found in the drier deserts of western India. They are rough-scaled, with enlarged forehead scales, well-developed limbs and show femoral pores. These are fast-moving and day-active predators of insects and other small invertebrates.

### Indian Fringe-toed Lizard *Acanthodactylus cantoris* 8cm

A lizard from sand dunes and other areas of sparse vegetation. Body large, slender; tail long; eyelids movable; lower eyelid translucent; lateral scales small; ventral scales smooth; toes long, fringed; dorsum of adults are reddish brown to grey, while juveniles are striped yellow and black, with blue tails. A swift-moving lizard from dry rocky, sandy or alluvial soil, including sea beaches. It excavates shallow burrows in such habitats. Its diet comprises grasshoppers, beetles, crickets and ants. Clutch size is 4–10, laid between late March and July, hatching taking place between late June and November. Known from Jammu and Kashmir, Punjab, Rajasthan and Uttar Pradesh States in northern and north-western India, as well as Pakistan and Afghanistan.

### Snake-eyed Lacerta *Ophisops jerdoni* 4.1cm

An inhabitant of dry, rocky terrain, this lizard avoids sandy habitats. Slender-bodied; head with large scales; limbs well-developed; forehead scales rough; dorsal scales smooth or weakly keeled; femoral pores present in both sexes; fringes on toes absent; dorsum brown or olive, darker on the sides; a white or yellow stripe along the side of the head, from eye to base of tail; another from upper lip to base of hindlimbs; belly white. Diurnal and terrestrial, found on rocky terrain, where they move with great speed. This species is known to bask communally and conceals itself under stones. Grasshoppers, beetles, ants, termites, caterpillars and spiders are consumed. Clutches comprise 2–7 eggs, measuring 4–5 × 7mm, laid between March and August, hatching taking place between July and November. Hatchlings measure 1.5–2cm. Known from Punjab, Rajasthan and Gujarat States of western India, and also adjacent regions of Pakistan.

## Leschenault's Lacerta *Ophisops leschenaultii* 5cm

A widespread species of lizard from the scrub forests and other types of open jungle of the Indian Peninsula south of the River Ganga. Slender-bodied; head with large scales; limbs well-developed; anterior lip scales and dorsal scales keeled; tail relatively long; dorsum brown or golden yellow, with paired black stripe from eye to sides of body and tail; a second along upper lip to side of body; tail and limbs reddish brown; belly unpatterned greenish cream. Diurnal, terrestrial and quick moving, it feeds on insects. Clutches of 6 eggs are produced in April. Widespread in northern India and Peninsular India, in addition to the northern part of Sri Lanka.

## Khasi Hills Long-tailed Lizard *Takydromus khasiensis* 5cm

An extremely long-tailed lizard inhabiting grasslands from northeastern India. Head rather long; dorsal surface with large, keeled, plate-like scales; sides of body with large, pointed and keeled scales; tail nearly three times as long as snout–vent length; femoral pores 2–3; dorsum brownish olive; a light dorso-lateral stripe between the eye to the base of tail, bordered above and below with black spots; a black streak along the head; belly greenish cream. Nothing is known of the diet or reproductive habits of this species. Known from Meghalaya, Mizoram and Assam States, as well as Bangladesh and northern Myanmar.

# SCINCIDAE (SKINKS)

Skinks are shiny-scaled, day-active lizards, found scurrying on the forest floor wherever there are patches of sunlight filtering in. This is one of largest families of lizards, and is found on all continents. They actively search for their prey on the surface of soil (a few species are arboreal), which comprises insects and other small invertebrates. Those that are fossorial are little known. Most skinks have smooth scales, possibly adapted for burrowing in soil, and all have detachable tails, that regenerate eventually.

### Ladakhi Rock Skink *Asymblepharus ladacensis* 6cm

A slender skink, with a 'clear window' in the lower eyelid, from the high Himalayas. Snout bluntly pointed; limbs with 5 fingers and toes; mid-dorsal scale rows 32–38; tail long, tapering to a fine point; dorsum bronze-brown, with dark flecks and scattered light-edged scales; a dark lateral stripe from eye to side of body that encloses white spots; belly bluish white. An alpine species found at high altitudes of up to 4,200m. Diurnal inhabitant of rocky environments, such as cliffs, rock walls and edges of rivers. Diet comprises insects. Presumably viviparous, like its close relatives. Widespread in appropriate habitats in Jammu and Kashmir State, Himachal Pradesh and Uttar Pradesh, as well as Nepal and Baltistan in northern Pakistan.

### Sikkimese Rock Skink *Asymblepharus sikimmensis* 5cm

Another slender skink, with a 'clear window' in the lower eyelid, from the high Himalayas. Snout bluntly pointed; limbs with 5 fingers and toes; mid-dorsal scale rows 22–24; tail long, tapering to a fine point; dorsum bronze-brown, with small black spots or short stripes arranged longitudinally; belly light blue or cream; a distinct dark brown stripe along the side of the body. Associated with rocky habitats, is diurnal and insectivorous. Clutches are laid in late June within damp moss in tree trunks, clutches comprising 3–6 (rarely 2 or 8) eggs, measuring 6 × 10mm. Hatchlings measure 3.7cm and emerge in July. Replaces its relatives in the Eastern Himalayas, with records being from Sikkim and northern West Bengal, and also an isolated locality in eastern Bihar State, as well as Nepal.

## Nicobarese Tree Skink *Dasia nicobarensis* 10cm

A small, olive-coloured tree skink endemic to the islands of the Nicobars. Body slender; ear-opening small; snout pointed; scales under tail enlarged; dorsum olive-brown, with a pale stripe along the sides of the body and tail base; belly bluish cream, each scale with a pale centre. Diurnal and arboreal, sometimes found on thatched huts, its diet is presumably insects but nothing else is known of its habits. Known only from Car Nicobar and Great Nicobar, in the Bay of Bengal.

## Olive Tree Skink *Dasia olivacea* 12cm

A relatively large, olive-coloured tree skink from the islands of the Nicobars, and also widespread in south-east Asia. Body more robust than the Nicobarese Tree Skink, from which it also differs in having scales under the tail not enlarged; ear-opening small; snout pointed; dorsum greenish brown, sometimes black-spotted; belly unpatterned cream. Juveniles are blackish brown, with yellow bands. Diurnal and arboreal, it dwells in large trees, especially at the edges of clearings, sheltering under peeling bark. Its diet comprises insects and clutches comprise up to 14 eggs; more than a single clutch may be produced in a year. Indian records are from the Nicobar Islands, in the Bay of Bengal; this species is widespread in Thailand and Peninsular Malaysia, as well as Sumatra and Borneo.

## Small-eared Striped Skink *Lipinia macrotympana* 4cm

A strikingly coloured, ground-dwelling skink, whose closest relatives are found in south-east Asia and the South Pacific. Body slender; head small, distinct from neck; snout acute; limbs rather small, tail elongated, rounded; ending in a sharp point; tympanum exposed, its borders lacking lobules; transparent disk on lower eyelid; dorsal scales smooth; ventral scales overlapping; dorsum with a yellow, vertebral stripe; paravertebral region with grey stripes; belly unpatterned cream, and also reportedly, red; tail bright orange. Diurnal and terrestrial, it has been found at the edge of sea beaches, bordering lowland rainforests. Its diet and other aspects of its natural history remain unknown, except that it produces 2 eggs at a time. This skink is found in the Andaman and Nicobar Islands in the Bay of Bengal.

## Bowring's Supple Skink *Lygosoma bowringii* 6cm

Another semi-fossorial skink with tiny limbs, the body nearly as thin as a match stick, found in the Bay Islands. Body elongate; head scarcely distinct from neck; lower eyelid scaly; ear-opening rounded; scales smooth or weakly keeled; tail rather thick, rounded, tapering to a narrow point; dorsum bronze-brown; the sides with a dark band, with white and black spots; belly unpatterned yellow; tail of juveniles bright red, becoming grey or brown with growth. Inhabits relatively open areas, and most commonly seen during the day in clearings and close to human habitation. Diet comprises small insects. Clutches of 2–4 eggs are produced at a time. Restricted within India to the Andaman and Nicobar Islands, this species is otherwise widespread in south-east Asia.

**Spotted Supple Skink** *Lygosoma punctata*  9cm

Yet another semi-fossorial, match-stick-thin skink with tiny limbs, it is frequently seen as it scuttles over leaf litter and frequently enters houses. Body elongate; head scarcely distinct from neck; lower eyelid with a transparent disk; ear-opening rounded; scales smooth; tail rather thick, rounded, tapering to a narrow point; dorsum bronze-brown, with 4–6 rows of black spots, the lateral ones more distinct; a broad cream stripe along the body; belly unpatterned cream; tail of juveniles bright red, becoming brown or pink with growth. Relatively common in the hills, although it also occurs in the plains. Diurnal, its diet comprises small insects. Clutches of 2–4 eggs. Widespread in India, and also Sri Lanka, Bangladesh and Pakistan.

**Andaman Grass Skink** *Mabuya andamanensis*  11cm

A fairly common, ground-dwelling skink from the Andaman Islands. Body robust; head scarcely distinct from neck; lower eyelids scaly; dorsal scales with 5–7 large keels; dorsum brown, with two series of black spots along the vertebral line; a dark stripe from the corner of the eyes that run to the front half of the sides of the body; belly yellowish cream. During the breeding season, the sides of the head, neck and belly are bright red. Diurnal and terrestrial, feeding on insects. Nothing is known of its reproductive biology. Known only from the Andaman Islands in the Bay of Bengal, including the Cocos group belonging to Myanmar.

## Keeled Grass Skink *Mabuya carinata* 13cm

The commonest skink. Body robust; lower eyelids scaly; dorsal scales with 3–8 keels; ventral scales smooth; dorsum bronze-brown or olive, with a yellow lateral band; a broad, chocolate-brown band on top; belly cream or yellow. During the breeding season, the sides of males turn bright red. Inhabits rainforests, deserts, scrub forests and parks and gardens of cities. Diurnal, and terrestrial, frequently seen basking or foraging in open areas. Crickets, caterpillars, beetles, earthworms and small vertebrates are consumed. Clutches include 2–8 eggs, 11–12 × 16–17mm, laid in a self-excavated hole or under fallen logs, between August and September; hatchlings emerge between May and June, 1.2–1.3cm. Widespread in India and Sri Lanka.

## Bronze Grass Skink *Mabuya macularia* 8cm

A small, forest skink, widespread in the plains and hills of India. Body slender; dorsal scales with 5–9 keels; dorsum bronzy brown, with or without spots, sides darker, spotted with white, especially in juveniles and in males, brown or grey in females; belly unpatterned cream; breeding males with bright red lips and flanks. Inhabits deciduous to evergreen forests, as well as plantations. Diet includes beetles and grasshoppers. Clutches comprise 2, rarely 1, eggs, 7–8 × 13–15mm, in the Western Ghats and central India, although clutches of 1–4 are also known elsewhere. Eggs are deposited under dead leaves or under logs, between June and September. More than 1 clutch laid annually. Besides India, this species occurs in Sri Lanka, Pakistan, Nepal, Bangladesh, Bhutan to mainland south-east Asia.

**Many-lined Grass Skink** *Mabuya multifasciata*  14cm

A familiar 'weed' species of lizard from south-east Asia that occurs in two different regions of India – the extreme north-east and the Bay Islands. Body large, robust; lower eyelid scaly; dorsal scales with 3, rarely 5, keels; dorsum bronze-brown, usually with a dark brown band, with a series of white spots or streaks along the sides of the body; during the breeding season, the males show a bright orange or reddish-orange side band; a pale, dorso-lateral line present; belly cream. Commonly seen in disturbed habitats, such as in clearings around human settlements, and also at forest edges. It is diurnal, terrestrial and insectivorous. Ovoviviparous, giving birth to 2–10 live young, measuring 3.6–4.3cm. Indian records are from Assam and Nagaland States, besides the Nicobar Islands, the species is widespread in south-east Asia and southern China.

**Four-keeled Grass Skink** *Mabuya quadricarinata*  5cm

George Robert Zug, National Museum of Natural History, Smithsonian Institution

A little-known, ground-dwelling lizard, with 4 sharp keels on the dorsal scales, from north-eastern India. Head indistinct from neck; lower eyelid scaly; dorsal scales with 4 distinct keels; dorsum olive-brown, unpatterned or with small, black spots that are arranged longitudinally; sides with or without dark lines; belly and upper lip cream. Presumably diurnal and an inhabitant of open forests and clearings. Nothing is known of its diet and reproductive habits. Known from Assam State, and also Myanmar.

## Lined Grass Skink *Mabuya rudis* 12cm

A rough-scaled, ground-dwelling skink known only from tropical islands. Head indistinct from neck; forehead scales at posterior rugose; dorsal scales with 3 strong keels; mid-dorsal scale rows typically 28–30; dorsum olive-brown, with a light-edged, dark brown line along the sides of the head and body; sides white-spotted; throat of adult males crimson; that of females, unpatterned cream; belly greenish white, the throat sometimes dark-spotted. Inhabits forested habitats, and is diurnal and terrestrial, feeding on insects. Clutches include 2–4 eggs. The Indian records are from Great Nicobar, in the Bay of Bengal, this species is also found in Borneo, Sumatra, Sulawesi and the Sulu Archipelago of the Philippines.

## Rough-backed Grass Skink *Mabuya rugifera* 7cm

A small, ground-dwelling forest lizard from the Nicobar Islands. Head indistinct from neck; lower eyelids scaly; dorsal scales with 5, rarely 7, distinct keels; dorsum blackish brown, with 5–7 greenish-cream, longitudinal stripes, that are sometimes broken up to form spots, giving it a grizzled appearance; belly greenish cream, throat dark-spotted. During the breeding season, the males acquire a bright red coloration on the sides of the throat. Inhabits forested areas in the mid-hills, and is diurnal and terrestrial, feeding on insects. Reproductive habits unknown. Within India, it is restricted to the Nicobar Islands in the Bay of Bengal, the species also occurring in southern Thailand, the Malay Peninsula, Sumatra, Java and Borneo.

## Tytler's Grass Skink *Mabuya tytleri* 15cm

A large-growing forest skink, with a robust body, restricted to the Andaman Islands. Head rather large, adults with swollen cheeks; lower eyelid scaly; dorsal scales with 3 weak keels, of which the central one is the least well-defined; dorsum bronze-brown, unpatterned or with darker spots; belly greenish cream. Inhabits lowland rainforests, and is diurnal and terrestrial, feeding on insects and other invertebrates. Reproductive habits unknown. Endemic to the Andaman Islands, in the Bay of Bengal.

## Indian Sandfish *Ophiomorus raithmai* 10cm

A slender, smooth-scaled and sharp-snouted skink with reduced limbs that inhabits sandy deserts, swimming in the sand, a habit which has earned it the vernacular name, Reg-Mahi ('Sandfish'). Head indistinct from neck; lower eyelid with a 'clear window'; fingers three; toes three; dorsum pale brown or yellowish brown; belly paler. Crepuscular and fossorial to surface-living, dwelling at the base of shrubs. Its characteristic sinuous tracts on the surface of the sand are the first indications of its presence. These skinks are most active during the spring and winter, remaining under the surface during the dry as well as wet seasons. They are predators of locusts, and also eat termites, moths, grasshoppers, cockroaches and beetles. Known from the arid western states of Gujarat and western Rajasthan, as well as adjacent areas of Pakistan.

## Beddome's Cat Skink *Ristella beddomii* 4cm

A little-known, dark, terrestrial and semi-fossorial skink from the Western Ghats. Snout short; body elongate; limbs reduced; tail cylindrical; claws can be retracted completely inside compressed sheaths of scales; mid-dorsal scale rows 26 or 28; dorsum reddish brown, scales with dark brown tips or on the centre of the scales; sides with indistinct dark lines and more prominent yellow spots; belly cream. Found in evergreen forests and moist semi-deciduous forests, on the forest floor, in such microhabitats as within leaf litter or on bare soil. Egg laying takes place during the south-western monsoons. Clutches include 3 eggs, of dimensions 6 × 9mm. Known from the central and southern portions of the Ghats, from Travancore, Tenmalai, Ponmudi and Parambikulam ranges of Kerala and Karnataka States.

## Travancore Cat Skink *Ristella travancoricus* 4cm

Another dark, terrestrial and semi-fossorial skink from the Western Ghats. Snout short; body elongate; limbs reduced; tail cylindrical; claws can be completely retracted inside compressed sheaths of scales; mid-dorsal scale rows 22, 24 or 26; dorsum reddish brown, the scales on the sides having dark brown tips or centres; a dark stripe or yellow spots on the sides sometimes present; belly cream. Inhabits evergreen forests, up to 950m, and active in the leaf litter. Egg laying takes place during the south-western monsoons. Clutches include 2 eggs, of dimensions 5–6 × 11mm, laid under rocks and dead leaves. Known from the Tirunelveli Hills of western Tamil Nadu State and Ponmudi Hills of Kerala State.

**Side-spotted Ground Skink** *Kaestlea laterimaculatum* 3.8cm

A beautiful, blue-tailed species of forest skink. A medium-sized species; lobules at edge of ears absent; loreals 5; fronto-parietals divided; mid-dorsal scale rows 20–25; 20–25 lamellae under fourth toe; dorsum bronze-brown, with a light-edged, black stripe along side of head and body; dark-spotted below; 2 black lines on dorsum along outer margins of vertebral series of scales; belly grey; tail blue. Diurnal and active on the forest floor. Diet unknown, and likely to be small insects. Nothing is known of its reproductive habits. Restricted to the Western Ghats, where it is known from the Nilgiris, Tirunelveli and Travancore regions of Tamil Nadu and Kerala States.

**Palni Hills Ground Skink** *Kaestlea palnicum* 4.7cm

An attractive, black-banded species of forest skink. A medium-sized species; lobules at edge of ears absent; mid-dorsal scale rows 28–30; lamellae under fourth toe 19; dorsum brown, with a light, dorso-lateral stripe along the side of the head and body; margined on inner side with dark brown; belly greyish white; tail brown. Diurnal and active on the forest floor. Diet unknown, and likely to be small insects. Nothing is known of its reproductive habits. Restricted to the Western Ghats, where it is known from the Palni Hills and Coimbatore in Tamil Nadu State.

## Reeves's Ground Skink *Scincella reevesi* 5cm

A ground-dwelling skink known from the low- and mid-hills of the Himalayas. Snout short; body slender; limbs somewhat reduced; eyes rather large; scales smooth; dorsum light or dark brown, with small black spots that may fuse to form a dark line; a black stripe along the sides, starting from the eyes; belly cream. Inhabits forested habitats at elevations up to 3,000m. Diurnal and terrestrial, its diet comprises insects. Reproductive habits remain unknown. Although not yet recorded from India, it may be found in the north-east, as it is known from Nepal as well as Myanmar, southern China, Thailand, Vietnam, Cambodia and Laos.

## Dussumier's Litter Skink *Sphenomorphus dussumieri* 6cm

A common, terrestrial skink from the mid-hills of the Western Ghats. Head distinct from neck; snout short; tympanum situated on the surface, not sunk; body slender; dorsal scales smooth, with fine striations; limbs relatively short; dorsum bronze-brown, with dark spots, a light, dorso-lateral stripe from the eyes to the sides of the body, its inner edge with a dark brown, white-spotted streak; a broad stripe on the sides that is edged with white below; belly cream. Inhabits evergreen, moist deciduous and plantation forests, such as rubber plantations, in closed as well as open forests. Diurnal, its diet and reproductive habits are unknown. Known from Karnataka and Kerala States.

## Himalayan Litter Skink *Sphenomorphus indicus* 9cm

A common, ground-dwelling skink from north-eastern India. Head distinct from neck; snout short; tympanum deeply sunk; body slender; dorsal scales smooth; dorsum brown, unpatterned or with dark brown spots arranged to form longitudinal lines; lips dark-barred; belly cream. Inhabits lowland evergreen forests, hiding in the leaf litter and under fallen trees. Diurnal, feeding on insects. Ovoviviparous, producing 4–11 young at a time. Distributed from Sikkim, northern West Bengal and Meghalaya States, and also Bhutan, to southern China, Tibet, Indo-China, Myanmar, Thailand and the Malay Peninsula.

## Spotted Litter Skink *Sphenomorphus maculatus* 6cm

A common, ground-dwelling skink from north-eastern India and the Andaman and Nicobar Islands. Head distinct from neck; snout short; tympanum on the surface, not deeply sunk; body slender; dorsal scales smooth; dorsum bronze-brown or brownish pink, unpatterned or with dark green spots; 2 dark median series of spots; a dark lateral band on the sides of the body, spotted with white; belly cream, turning yellow during the breeding season. Diurnal and terrestrial, occurring from the plains, including seashores and edges of mangrove swamps, to the mid-hills. Diet comprises spiders, crickets and moths. Oviparous, producing 4–5 eggs at a time. Besides Sikkim, northern West Bengal, eastern Bihar and Assam States, in north-eastern India, this species occurs in the Andaman and Nicobar Islands, eastwards to southern China, Myanmar and Thailand.

**North-eastern Water Skink** *Tropidophorus assamensis* 4cm

*Samraat Pawar*

A little-known skink from mountain streams of north-eastern India. Head rather small; snout pointed; body elongate; tympanum at the surface; lower eyelid scaly; preanal scales greatly enlarged; dorsum brown, with light and dark markings; 2 broad, dark-edged, yellow dorsal cross-bars, one across the shoulders, one across the base of tail; tail dark-barred; belly light brown, with dark, longitudinal streaks. Inhabits edges of small, rocky streams in the low hills, into which they dive to escape predators and to hunt. Known from Mizoram State as well as north-eastern Bangladesh.

# UROMASTYCIDAE (SPINY-TAILED LIZARDS)

Spiny-tailed lizards of North Africa, the Middle East and south Asia and the butterfly lizards of south-east Asia, which were formerly placed in the family Agamidae. They inhabit open areas, such as scrub forests and sea beaches, are largely herbivorous and dwell in colonies in burrows excavated in the soil.

**Hardwicke's Spiny-tailed Lizard** *Uromastyx hardwickii* 35cm

*Close-up of head*           *Captives, for oil extraction*

A heavy-tailed lizard. Body depressed, lacking a crest and throat sac; tail thick at base, short, depressed, covered with large, spinose scales; dorsum yellowish brown; belly cream. Inhabits deserts and scrub forests. Diurnal and terrestrial, they burrow in compact and rocky soils, up to 3m. A colony may comprise 50 or more adults. Diet is a mixture of plant and animal matter, including grasses and insects. Eggs 20–30mm, and clutches of up to 15 laid between April and May. Western India, including Gujarat and Rajasthan, also, eastern Pakistan. Large numbers are caught for its valuable fat.

# VARANIDAE (MONITORS)

Monitors are the largest of the living lizards. They are swift and active predators of small mammals, birds, bird eggs, reptiles, amphibians and invertebrates. Their forked tongue, which is flicked in and out to taste the chemical nature of the environment, is reminiscent of snakes. The Water Monitor is one of the three largest lizards in the world, and is known to congregate on turtle nesting beaches to eat eggs and hatchlings. They are day-active, and forage on land, as well as in water, and some species frequently climb trees in search of bird eggs and nestlings.

**Bengal Monitor** *Varanus bengalensis* 1.74m

A lizard famous in Indian history for its reported use by Maratha heroes in scaling the walls of Mughal fortresses. Medium-sized monitor; snout somewhat elongated; nostrils nearer the eye than the snout-tip; nostril an oblique slit; nuchal scale rounded; crown scales larger than nuchal scales; mid-ventral scales smooth; tail flattened; juveniles pale or dark dorsally, with yellow bands comprising spots in transverse series; snout unpatterned; belly cream or yellow, lacking dark vertical V-shaped marks extending to sides of belly. Inhabits a variety of habitats, from semi-deserts and scrub to evergreen forests and plantations. Diet consists of a variety of insects and spiders, snails, crabs, frogs, small mammals, birds, lizards and snakes, in addition to carrion. Eggs may be laid in termitaria during the wet season, which in south-eastern India is in December and in northern India is August to September. Up to 12 may be laid, measuring 15 × 29mm. Hatchlings measure 9cm. Widespread in India; the range of the species extends from Afghanistan to Myanmar and includes Pakistan, Sri Lanka, Bangladesh and Nepal. Once considered a subspecies of this species, the South-east Asian Land Monitor (*Varanus nebulosus*) is here considered a distinct species.

## Yellow Monitor *Varanus flavescens* 83cm

A relatively small, brightly coloured monitor lizard from agricultural fields and wetlands. Snout short and convex, nostril an oblique slit, closer to snout tip than to orbit; nuchal scale strongly keeled; crown scales smaller than nuchals; mid-ventral scales smooth; tail strongly compressed; juveniles with transverse rows of fused yellow spots on a dark background, becoming less bright with growth; dorsum light to dark brown, rarely black, many with brownish-red to deep-red areas between yellow transverse bands; colour change occurs in adults of both sexes seasonally, when individuals have more orange-red suffusion on body. Insects, earthworms, amphibian and reptile eggs, birds and bird eggs and rodents are eaten. Nesting takes place during the south-west monsoons in August, when clutches of 4–30 eggs, measuring 21 × 37mm, are laid. Incubation period is 149–155 days. Associated with low-lying wetlands of the Indus–Ganga–Brahmaputra drainages.

## Desert Monitor *Varanus griseus* 1.33m

A medium-sized species of monitor from deserts and other arid regions. Snout depressed; nostril an oblique slit, nearer to eye than tip of snout; nuchal scale conical; crown scales larger than nuchal scales; ventral scales smooth, tail rounded or only slightly compressed; dorsum brown, snout lacking black bars; belly yellow. Inhabits deserts, semi-deserts and scrub forests and forages at dawn and at dusk. Diet consists of lizards, such as skinks, agamids and lacertids, and also beetles, small rodents, birds, snakes and turtles, and eggs of birds and reptiles. It is also known to scavenge. Clutches comprise 5 eggs that are produced in October; eggs leathery-shelled, hatching in July. Incubation period is 284 days. Distributed over the north-western part of India, including Rajasthan State. The range of the species extends from the Middle East, through Pakistan, to north-western India.

**Water Monitor** *Varanus salvator* 2.50m

An enormous species of monitor, associated with wetlands, such as mangrove swamps. Snout depressed; nostril rounded or oval, twice as far from the orbit as from the snout tip; nuchal scale strongly keeled; crown scales larger than nuchal scales; mid-ventral scales feebly keeled; tail strongly compressed with a double-toothed crest above; juveniles dark dorsally, yellow spotted or ocelli in transverse series; snout black-barred, especially on lips; belly yellow with narrow, black vertical V-shaped marks extending to sides of belly. The largest of the Indian monitors, and widespread in mangrove swamps and evergreen forests. Semi-aquatic, inhabiting marshes, estuaries, rivers and canals in cities, mangroves and dipterocarp forests. Insects, fishes, crabs, adult freshwater turtles, eggs of waterbirds, crocodiles and sea turtles, mouse-deer, in addition to carrion, are consumed. Clutches of 7–30 are produced between May and October, eggs measure 32–43 × 67–83mm, incubation period 8–9 months. Hatchlings measure 25–28.5cm. Abundant in the Sunderbans of West Bengal and Bhitarkanika of Orissa, as well as the Andaman and Nicobar Islands, and in evergreen forests of north-eastern India, including the states of Assam, Meghalaya and Nagaland. Also, Bangladesh, Sri Lanka, east to Indo-Malaya, Indo-China, southern China and the Philippines.

# CROCODYLIDAE (CROCODILES)

India is home to two species of true crocodiles, one from saltwater habitats, one from freshwater. They are predators of small to large-sized prey, and some large-growing individuals may pose a danger to humans and livestock. All species are linked to wetlands, such as rivers, lakes, dams and mangroves, and lay eggs. The sex of all crocodiles is determined by the incubation temperature of the eggs.

## Mugger Crocodile *Crocodylus paluster* 5.00m

*Basking adult*

*Close-up of head*      *Hatchling*

A large-growing freshwater crocodile; larger individuals can be dangerous to man. Snout relatively broad and heavy, forehead concave, ridges in front of the eyes absent; dorsal scales in 16–17 rows on trunk; postoccipital scutes absent; teeth includes 13–14 pairs of teeth on upper jaw and 14–15 pairs on lower jaw; juveniles light tan or brown with dark cross-bands on body and tail, while adults are grey to brown, usually without dark bands. Inhabits freshwater, from rivers to lakes, dams and reservoirs, generally far from tidal influence. Insects and small vertebrates, including fish and frogs are consumed by juveniles, while adults eat mammals as large as deer and goats, as well as smaller mammals, water birds, fish, snakes, lizards and turtles. This is a hole-nesting crocodile, laying 10–50 eggs at a time, and 2 clutches of eggs may be produced during a nesting season, at least in captivity. Eggs measure 39–51 × 64–84mm. The sex of crocodiles is determined by the incubation temperature of the eggs, unlike in mammals and birds. Widespread in India, the range of the species extends from eastern Iran, to Pakistan, India, Nepal and Bangladesh and Sri Lanka. In the past, hunting for skins and alteration of habitats have reduced populations of the species.

### Saltwater Crocodile *Crocodylus porosus* 6.20m

A large crocodile, responsible for a number of human mortalities. Snout heavy, with a pair of ridges running from orbit to centre of snout. Inhabits estuaries and mangroves. Diet includes crabs, shrimps, fish, reptiles, birds and mammals. Constructs a mound-nest, in which 60–80 eggs are deposited. Sunderbans and Bhitarkanika mangroves, as well as the Andaman and Nicobar Islands. Sri Lanka and Seychelles to Australia and the South Pacific.

## GAVIALIIDAE (THE GHARIAL)

The family of Gharials is represented by a single living species, although several fossil species indicate that they were once widespread. The Gharial is a specialized fish-eating crocodilian, found in the larger rivers in the Indian region.

### Gharial *Gavialis gangeticus* 7.00m

A large, fish-eating crocodilian. Snout slender, parallel-sided, tip with a distinctive knob in adult males; about 100 sharp, interlocking teeth; dorsum olive to tan; belly pale, with dark blotches or bands on dorsum. Inhabits large rivers in northern India, it is a specialized fish-eater, but apparently also scavenges. Nests on sand banks or alluvial deposits, laying 7–60 eggs at a time, eggs 59–64mm and hatch in 62 days. Hatchlings 17–18cm. Restricted to the Indus, Ganga, Brahmaputra and Mahanadi of northern and eastern India, besides Pakistan, Nepal and Bangladesh. There is a single unsubstantiated record from Ayeyarwaddy River of Myanmar and is at present extinct from Bhutan.

# BATAGURIDAE (ASIAN POND TURTLES)

These are hardshelled, primarily aquatic, although a few are terrestrial, showing large scales on their limbs as well as a 'high walk', like tortoises. The shell bears scutes and the snout lacks the piglike tubular structure seen in softshell turtles. There is a general tendency towards herbivory, although some are specialized feeders of fish and crustaceans, and a few show enlarged heads and associated jaw muscles for tackling hard-bodied prey such as molluscs. Eggs are hardshelled, elongated, and buried along banks of water bodies. Batagurid turtles are essentially distributed over tropical Asia, and many are exploited for food.

## River Terrapin *Batagur baska* 60cm

A large turtle from the mouths of rivers, especially flooded mangrove forests of eastern India. Carapace domed, heavily buttressed; long plastron; head small with an upturned snout; forehead covered with small scales; four claws on each forelimb; carapace olive-grey or brown, head similar coloured but lighter on sides, plastron unpatterned yellow. Occurs in mouths of rivers that are under tidal influence and mangrove-dominated. Fruits of *Sonneratia* are an important food item; leaves, stems and fruits are also consumed, besides molluscs, crustaceans and fish. River Terrapins in the Sunderbans nest on the sea coast. A clutch comprises 19–37 eggs, measuring 40 × 68mm; incubation period between 61–66 days. In India, the species is restricted to estuaries such as the Sunderbans, Bhitarkanika and the mouth of the Subarnarekha River. Also, coastal regions of Bangladesh, Myanmar, Thailand, the Malay Peninsula, Sumatra (in Indonesia), Cambodia and Vietnam. Endangered by overexploitation of eggs and adults for food, and habitat destruction. A captive breeding centre for this species exists in the Sunderbans.

# Malayan Box Turtle *Cuora amboinensis* 22cm

(Above) *Carapace and head;* (inset) *plastron*

Plastron with a well-developed plastral hinge, allowing complete closure of shell. Shell high-domed and smooth, with a single keel; carapace olive, brown or nearly black; plastron yellow or cream, with a single black blotch; face yellow-striped. Inhabits rivers, lakes, marshes, mangrove swamps, and rice fields. Primarily herbivorous, feeding on water plants and fungi; worms and aquatic insects also eaten. Clutches comprise 1–6 eggs and 2 clutches are laid a year; eggs 25–34 × 40–55mm and hatch 45–90 days later. Assam, Nagaland and Arunachal Pradesh, the Nicobar Islands; also Bangladesh, Myanmar, Thailand, Indo-China, Indo-Malaya and the Philippines.

# Oldham's Leaf Turtle *Cyclemys oldhami* 25cm

Shell leaf-like in shape and colour, presumably for camouflage with leaf litter. Shell oval, depressed, bearing three keels; enlarged scales on forehead; plastron with a hinge in adult turtles around 23–25cm in shell length; carapace and plastron are brown, with dark radiating lines. Inhabits lowhills and the plains, although more common at lower elevations, occurring in small rivers, streams as well as in ponds. Omnivorous, ingesting figs as well as invertebrates. Nests are dug in the ground, where 2–4 elongated hard-shelled eggs are laid. These hatch about 75 days later. Distributed from northern West Bengal, through Assam, Meghalaya, Mizoram and Arunachal Pradesh, besides Bangladesh, to southern China and Indo-China.

## Spotted Pond Turtle *Geoclemys hamiltonii* 41cm

A turtle with an enlarged head for cracking open mollusc shells. Carapace with three interrupted keels; head massive, with a short snout; shell black with yellow streaks and wedge-shaped marks; head black, with yellow spots, neck grey with cream spots. Inhabits ox-bow lakes and other standing bodies of water. Diet includes molluscs, grasses, fruits and leaves. More than a single clutch can be laid in a year, each comprising 13–24 eggs, which are brittle hardshelled, 24–28 × 41–51mm. Incubation period 23–76 days. It occurs in the northern plains of India in the drainages of the Indus, Ganga and Brahmaputra, its distribution including Pakistan, Nepal and Bangladesh.

## Cochin Forest Cane Turtle *Vijayachelys silvatica* 13cm

Shekar Dattatri

The smallest Indian turtle. Carapace depressed, tricarinate and oval; head large; upper-jaw strongly hooked; eyes large; adult males typically darker and more brilliantly coloured than females and juveniles, carapace olive-brown, plastron yellow, sometimes with dark brown blotches on bridge, forehead black, snout and postocular stripe; female carapace reddish grey, plastron yellow with scattered dark pigments along seams; head with a pink postocular stripe and orange iris. Terrestrial, inhabiting evergreen, semi-evergreen and moist deciduous forests of the Western Ghats, between 400–800m altitude. Millipedes, snails, insects and leaves comprise its diet in the wild. Two eggs are laid, these are brittle shelled, 23–24 × 44–45mm. Confined to Kerala, Karnataka and western Tamil Nadu States, in south-western India.

**Crowned River Turtle** *Hardella thurjii* 61cm (female); 18cm (male)

Males of this turtle are a third of the size of the females. Carapace domed, vertebral keel interrupted; carapace dark brown with a grey-black vertebral keel; a yellowish-orange band usually present; plastron yellow, each scute with a large, dark blotch; four yellowish-orange stripes along face. Inhabits slow-moving rivers, marshes, estuaries and large bodies of water. Eggs laid September to January, clutch size 8–13 and a female may lay 30–100 eggs per season. Eggs elongated, 28–36 × 40–56mm. Incubation period up to 273 days. Hatchlings 4.1–4.6cm. Widespread in the drainages of the Indus, Ganga and Brahmaputra, in northern and north-eastern India.

**Three-striped Roofed Turtle** *Batagur dhongoka* 48cm

A large river turtle, highly valued for food. Carapace elevated, oval; vertebral keel terminates in a knob on the third vertebral; carapace brownish grey, with dark stripes on vertebral and pleural regions and marginal edges; plastron yellow; head and neck greyish cream, with a cream or yellow stripe across face. Inhabits large and medium-sized rivers. Males omnivorous, feeding on waterplants and molluscs, while females are vegetarian. Clutches of 21–35 eggs are produced March to April; eggs, 32–41 × 52–66mm, hatch in 56–89 days. Found in the Rivers Ganga and Chambal, and Nepal and Bangladesh.

# Painted Roofed Turtle *Batagur kachuga* 56cm

(Above) *male;* (inset) *female*

A rare and beautiful river turtle. Carapace moderately domed, oval, brownish-olive in males, dark brown or black in females; plastron of both sexes cream or yellow; adult males with blue-black head, a broad red patch on forehead, two yellow stripes on sides of head and six red stripes on a cream-coloured neck; adult females with yellow or silvery mandibles and dark brownish-black heads. Restricted to large rivers. Basks on sandbanks, rocks and logs. Feeds on water-plants. Eggs laid March to April, and also perhaps December. Clutch size 11–30 eggs, 38–46 × 64–75mm. Found in northern India.

# Tricarinate Hill Turtle *Melanochelys tricarinata* 16cm

A small, terrestrial turtle from the foot of the Himalayas. Carapace rather elongate, tricarinate, keels low; shell arched with steep sides; snout short; carapace dark olive, grey-black or reddish brown, with pale yellow keels, plastron yellow or orange, head and limbs grey-black; yellow or red stripe on face. Terrestrial, inhabiting grasslands along the Ganga and Brahmaputra as well as the hilly country in their vicinity. Crepuscular and omnivorous. Clutch size 1–3, eggs 23–25 × 38–44mm, produced February to April and October to December, hatch after 60–72 days. Widespread, from Uttaranchal, Uttar Pradesh and Bihar, through northern West Bengal to Assam and Arunachal Pradesh; also adjacent regions of Nepal and Bangladesh.

# Indian Black Turtle *Melanochelys trijuga* 38cm

*Subspecies* coronata

*Subspecies* thermalis

One of the most widespread as well as abundant turtles in Peninsular India. Carapace elongated, fairly high in adults, depressed in juveniles, tricarinate; carapace brown, plastron usually dark with a pale yellow border that may be lost in old specimens; head colour variable, and forms the basis of subspecific differentiation. Inhabits standing waters with aquatic vegetation, although it may also be found in rivers and other lotic habitats. Diet includes freshwater prawns, grass, water hyacinth, fruits, and also scavenges a long distance from water. Clutch size between 3-6, eggs 40-53 x 25-29 mm. Widespread in peninsular and north-eastern India; also Sri Lanka, Maldives, Nepal, Bangladesh, Myanmar and Thailand.

# Indian Eyed Turtle *Morenia petersi* 20cm

A domed turtle from slow-moving and stagnant water bodies. Carapace smooth, with a low vertebral keel; head small, with a pointed snout; carapace green, olive or grey-black, vertebrals and costals with a green or yellow border; first four vertebrals with green stripes and sometimes, a U-shaped mark; costals typically with pale green circles and looped lines; plastron with black blotches on axillary scute and some adjacent marginals; head olive with three yellow stripes on face. Inhabits slow-moving waters from both the Terai and Bhabar tracts at the foothills of the Himalayas. Nests are laid between the end of December and the end of January, on loamy soil with sparse vegetation. Clutch includes 6–10, eggs, 20 × 49mm, hatching between April and May. Isolated localities from Uttar Pradesh, Bihar, West Bengal and Assam, and also Bangladesh and Nepal.

**Brown Roofed Turtle** *Pangshura smithii* 22cm (female); 13cm (male)

A low-domed, pale roofed turtle from northern India. Shell elliptical, arched; medial keel weak, raised at posterior of vertebral scute; carapace light green (males) or brown (females), plastron and bridge yellow with a single, large blotch on scute; head yellowish grey or pinkish grey, with distinct brick-red patch on temple; neck grey, with yellow stripes; limbs grey. Restricted to large and medium-sized rivers and their vegetation-choked backwaters. Both water plants and fish are consumed. Clutch size 7–9, eggs elongated, brittle hardshelled, 22–25 × 40–42mm. Hatchling 3.6cm. Widespread from Punjab, Uttar Pradesh, Bihar, West Bengal and Assam, and also adjacent regions of Nepal, Bangladesh and Pakistan.

**Assam Roofed Turtle** *Pangshura sylhetensis* 20cm

A tiny turtle with a highly elevated shell. Shell strongly elevated, giving it a spike-like appearance, especially in juveniles, serrated posteriorly; the only Indian freshwater turtle with 13 marginals; snout slightly projecting; carapace olive-brown with a pale brown, vertebral keel, plastron with large, black blotches; red stripes on face. Inhabits hill streams, ox-bow lakes and low-lying marshes in the plains as well as evergreen forests. Carnivorous and apparently crepuscular. Clutches comprise 5 eggs produced in March. Restricted to northern West Bengal, Assam, Arunachal Pradesh and Meghalaya States, as well as Bangladesh.

# Indian Roofed Turtle *Pangshura tectum* 18cm

A small, brightly coloured roofed turtle from ponds and other standing bodies of water. Carapace elevated, oval, with distinct vertebral keel on third vertebral that is spike-like, especially in juveniles; head small with a projecting snout; upper jaw unnotched; serrated carapace brownish olive, with light brown, red or orange stripe along first three vertebral scutes; marginals with a narrow yellow border; plastron yellow or pink, with 2–4 black markings on plastral scutes; head with orange or red crescentic-shaped postocular markings, curving up from below eyes to meet on forehead; neck dark grey with thin, yellow or cream stripes. Inhabits standing waters. Basks communally, and several turtles are usually seen basking on logs on sides of rivers. Clutch size between 4-11, eggs 37-45 x 21-24mm. Distributed in northern India, besides Pakistan, Nepal and Bangladesh.

# Indian Tent Turtle *Pangshura tentoria* 27cm

*Subspecies* flaviventris

*Subspecies* circumdata

A small roofed turtle, widespread in northern and central India. Carapace elevated, oval, with a distinct vertebral keel on third vertebral; plastron truncated anteriorly, notched posteriorly; forelobe of plastron much shorter than bridge, head small with projecting snout; upper jaw unnotched; serrated; with a single V-shaped ridge; digits entirely webbed; third and fourth vertebrals longer than wide; fifth vertebral wider than long; first and second vertebrals longer than wide or wider than long; forehead with irregular scales; coloration variable, shell olive dorsally, and pinkish-yellow belly either unpatterned or with a single, black blotch on each scute. Clutch size between 3-12, eggs 43-50 x 26-29mm. Widely distributed in India, reaching the central part of the Peninsula, and also the northern and north-eastern parts; also Bangladesh, Nepal and Pakistan. Occasionally captured for food.

## Keeled Box Turtle *Cuora mouhotii* 18cm

A strikingly flat-topped turtle from north-eastern India. Shell elongated, carapace flat-topped, 3 prominent keels on carapace; weak hinge across plastron in adult females; carapace dark or light brown, and plastron yellow or light brown. Inhabits evergreen hill forests. Omnivorous. Clutch comprises 1–5 eggs, large and brittle-shelled, 25–27 × 40–56mm, hatching in 90–101 days. Distributed in Assam, Mizoram, Manipur, Meghalaya and Arunachal Pradesh; also Myanmar, northern Thailand, Laos, Cambodia and eastern China.

# CHELONIIDAE (MARINE TURTLES)

All but one species of marine turtles belong to this family. They are exclusively marine in habit, only the adult females coming ashore to lay eggs. Widespread in the warm seas of the world, marine turtles are threatened by a variety of human activities, from hunting for their flesh and shell scutes, to pollution of marine habitats and destruction of nesting beaches.

## Loggerhead Sea Turtle *Caretta caretta* 1.20m

A large sea turtle with a massive head. Carapace elongated, with a tapering end; 3–4 infralabial scutes that lack pores; 13 marginal scutes; carapace reddish brown, plastron yellowish brown or yellowish orange. Often confused with the Olive Ridley Sea Turtle, this species can be differentiated in having 5 (rather than 6) costals; bridge with 3 (not 4) inframarginals; and carapace reddish brown (versus olive-green or greyish olive). Inhabits warm, subtropical seas, from bays, lagoons and estuaries. Diet comprises molluscs and crustaceans, the large jaws adapted to crush their shells. Eggs 35–55mm, 23–178 eggs being laid at a time, hatching 49–80 days later. This is the rarest of the Indian marine turtles, known only from the Gulf of Mannar.

## Green Turtle *Chelonia mydas* 1.40m

A large sea turtle, so called for the colour of its fat, once used for making turtle soup. Carapace heart-shaped; scutes of carapace not overlapping; upper jaw lacking a hook; forelimbs with a single claw; carapace olive or brown, usually with a dark radiating pattern, plastron pale yellow; adult males smaller than females and possess relatively longer tails than females that project out of the rim of the carapace. Widely distributed in tropical regions, around oceanic islands and along coasts with wide sandy beaches. Juveniles carnivorous, adults consume seagrass and seaweeds. Eggs are softshelled, spherical, each nest containing 98–172 eggs, 41–42mm, that hatch 60 days later. Up to 11 nests may be laid by a female within a nesting season. Within Indian waters, the turtle is most common on the west coast, such as Gujarat State and the Andaman Islands.

## Hawksbill Sea Turtle *Eretmochelys imbricata* 1.00m

Another large sea turtle, its scutes in demand for making tortoiseshell items. Carapace heart-shaped; scutes of carapace with 4 pairs of imbricate (overlapping) costal scutes; 2 pairs of prefrontal scales; upper jaw relatively narrow, elongate; upper jaw forward projecting; carapace olive-brown, juveniles with darker blotches. Associated with reefs, bays, estuaries and lagoons, its almost exclusive diet of sponges make it remarkable among sea turtles; algae, corals and shellfish also consumed. Nesting varies with locality – August and January in the Andamans; June and October on the Indian mainland. Clutch size also varies from one locality to another, and may be 96–177; eggs spherical, 30–35mm, take 57–65 days to hatch. Although recorded from both coasts of Peninsular India, it is nowhere abundant, with significant local nesting population only on the Andaman Islands.

## Olive Ridley Sea Turtle *Lepidochelys olivacea* 80cm

The smallest Indian sea turtle. Carapace broad, heart-shaped, posterior marginals serrated, with juxtaposed costal scutes; 5 to 9 pairs of costals; bridge with 4 inframarginals, each with a pore; adult shell smooth; carapace olive-green or greyish olive; plastron greenish yellow; juveniles grey-black dorsally; cream ventrally. Some of the largest nesting aggregations (referred to as 'arribadas') occur in Orissa, where several hundred thousand turtles congregate to nest. Other major nesting sites are on the west coast and on the Andaman Islands. Clutches comprise 50–160 eggs, 34–43mm; incubation period 45–60 days. Hatchlings 3.8–5.0cm.

## DERMOCHELYIDAE
## (LEATHERBACK SEA TURTLE)

This family includes a single living species, which is the largest living turtle, and one of the heaviest living reptiles. It frequently wanders into cold Arctic waters, presumably in search of jellyfish.

## Leatherback Sea Turtle *Dermochelys coriacea* 2.56m

The largest and heaviest living reptile, this turtle is known to weigh up to 916kg. The shell is elongated and tapered towards the posterior, bearing 7 ridges on carapace and 5 on the plastron; shell skin-clad in adults; distinct scale-like structures on hatchling shells; limbs paddle-like, clawless. Widely distributed, it inhabits the open ocean. The Leatherback feeds primarily on jellyfish, to capture which, it can dive down to 1,200m. Nests are excavated on beaches with uninterrupted open access from deep waters. Clutches comprise 90–130 eggs, which are spherical, soft-shelled, 5.0–5.4cm. Indian records of this species are mostly from the Andaman and Nicobar Islands, with isolated mainland records.

# TESTUDINIDAE (LAND TORTOISES)

The true tortoises are almost entirely herbivorous (although almost all will scavenge on carrion from time to time), recognizable in possessing columnar legs, rounded shells and heavy scales on limbs. They are adapted for a life on dry land, and many species can survive long periods without water. A few species from wetter parts of range are, however, fond of water, wallowing in forest streams for hours. Tortoises are known dispersal agents of forest plants. Popular in the pet trade, large numbers are gathered for export.

## Indian Star Tortoise *Geochelone elegans* 38cm

(Above) *Adult;* (left) *mating*

An unmistakable land tortoise, with a star-like pattern on both the carapace and plastron. Shell elongated in adults, rounded in juveniles; domed dorsally with flattened sides; weak bicuspid or tricuspid upper jaw; several distinct conical tubercles on thigh; carapace and plastron star-marked with a pattern of dark brown or black on yellow or beige, superimposed dark colour especially prominent in juveniles. Found primarily in scrub forests and edges of deserts, agricultural fields, forests of teak, grasslands and thorn scrub. Largely herbivorous, known to eat flowers of various species of plants, although also known to scavenge on animal matter. Nesting season coincides with the monsoons. Eggs are hard, brittle-shelled, generally ellipsoidal, laid in mid-November in western India, and March–June and October–January in south-eastern India. Clutch size is 1–10 and egg dimensions are 31–37 × 40–51mm. Incubation period is 47–178 days. Restricted to the dry regions of north-western India and south-eastern and southern India, in addition to extreme eastern Pakistan and northern and eastern Sri Lanka. Several aboriginal communities hunt these animals for local consumption, including the Irulas of Tamil Nadu and the Palaiyars of North Travancore. Threatened by the pet trade and through habitat destruction.

## Elongated Tortoise *Indotestudo elongata* 33cm

A dark-spotted tortoise from eastern and northern India. Carapace domed, highest point in vertebral III, plastron elongated, with a deep notch posteriorly; limbs heavily scaled, nuchal scute long and narrow; shell yellowish brown or olive, with scattered black blotches, plastron sometimes unpatterned. Inhabits deciduous forests and evergreen forests, including forests of sal and teak. Primarily herbivorous, its diet includes leaves, flowers, fruits, fungi, occasionally scavenging on animal matter. Eggs spherical or elongated, 1–7 per clutch, 37 × 50mm. Incubation period 96–165 days. Hatchlings 4.9cm. Eastern and north-eastern India; also Nepal, Bangladesh, Indo-China and Indo-Malaya.

## Travancore Tortoise *Indotestudo travancorica* 33cm

*Hatchling*    *Carapace*

Another dark-spotted tortoise with a spotted shell, from the Western Ghats. Shell elongated; nuchal absent; tail ends in claw-like spur; shell olive or brown, usually with black blotches on each scute. Restricted to moist evergreen and semi-evergreen forests to an altitude of at least 450m. Largely herbivorous, with grass, fungi, bamboo shoots, fallen fruits, flowers and also insects and frogs ingested. Copulation takes place at the onset of monsoons. Clutches are 1–3, eggs 31–44 × 40–58mm. Incubation period 146–149 days and hatchlings 5.5–6.0cm. The range of the species encompasses the states of Kerala, Karnataka and western Tamil Nadu.

### Asian Giant Tortoise *Manouria emys* 50cm

This is the largest of the land tortoises, weighing up to 20 kilos. Shell relatively low; vertebral region depressed; distinct growth rings on scutes of the carapace; outer surface of forelimbs bears large scales; a pair of tuberculate scales on thighs; shell blackish brown; plastron lighter. Largely herbivorous, although insects and frogs are also eaten. Constructs a mound nest by sweeping leaf litter in which 23–51 hardshelled, spherical eggs, 51–54mm, are deposited. Thereafter, it guards the nest, attacking egg predators. Hatchlings 6.0–6.6cm and take 60–75 days to emerge. Evergreen forests of north-eastern India, including Assam, Meghalaya and Nagaland; also, southern China, Indo-China and Indo-Malaya, including Sumatra and Borneo.

## TRIONYCHIDAE (SOFTSHELL TURTLES)

A skin-clad shell, just three claws on each limb and nostrils set on a fleshy proboscis immediately set these turtles apart from all others. Highly aquatic, they are found in rivers and ponds, and are primarily carnivorous, although waterplants may also be consumed. Softshell turtles are aggressive, and can deliver a painful bite, so even hatchlings need to be handled with caution.

### Malayan Softshell Turtle *Amyda cartilaginea* 70cm

The Malayan Softshell Turtle has been reported recently from Mizoram State in north-eastern India. Snout longer than eye; a distinct row of tubercles along the front of the carapace; head dark olive, bearing numerous indistinct yellowish-cream spots; upper part of shell is greenish grey or olive, sometimes with black spots, which tend to disappear with growth; plastron with 5 callosities. In adult males, tail is relatively longer, exceeding rim of carapace. In addition, plastron is white in males, grey in females. This species is carnivorous and active at night, when it hunts fish, frogs, shrimps and water insects along streams. Nests are holes in river banks, where 4–8 rounded eggs, measuring 21–33mm in diameter, are deposited. Eggs hatch in 130–140 days. Besides north-eastern India, this turtle is known from mainland south-east Asia, besides the islands of Sumatra, Java and Borneo. Locally hunted for food.

# Indian Softshell Turtle *Nilssonia gangeticus* 94cm

A large, aggressive softshell turtle. Carapace low and oval; carapace grey-green, usually with darker reticulations; eye-like markings on dorsum of juveniles yellow-bordered; head green dorsally, with black, oblique stripes on forehead and temples. Inhabits rivers, ponds, lakes and reservoirs. Omnivorous, consuming waterplants, invertebrates and vertebrates, and also scavenges on carrion. Known to grab waterfowl from beneath the surface of water and when in small groups, even to attack the Nilgai (or Blue Bull, a large antelope). Eggs spherical, brittle hardshelled, 30–35mm, and between 13–35 eggs are laid. Distribution includes northern India, Nepal, Pakistan and Bangladesh.

# Indian Peacock Softshell Turtle *Nilssonia hurum* 60cm

A beautiful softshell turtle, marked with bright colours on head. Shell with longitudinal rows of tubercles on anterior of carapace; carapace olive with yellow rim, juveniles with 4–6 dark-rimmed, yellow-bordered ocelli; plastron light grey; forehead with black reticulations and large orange or yellow patches, across snout and on sides. Inhabits rivers, lakes, ponds and reservoirs. Snails, fish and larvae of mosquito are consumed. Nests between August–December, in clayey–sandy soil. Eggs spherical, hardshelled, 20–38. Records from India are from the larger rivers of northern and eastern India, as well as isolated freshwater bodies in the region, in addition to Bangladesh and Nepal.

## Leith's Softshell Turtle *Nilssonia leithii* 64cm

A large turtle from rivers and reservoirs. Carapace low and oval; snout relatively long; patch of flat, wart-like tubercles present on front of carapace and along midline; carapace grey or greyish olive with yellow vermiculations; juveniles with 4–6 dark-centred, light bordered, eye-like spots; head greenish grey, sometimes with a black streak from eye to neck. Inhabits rivers and reservoirs. Diet includes fish, crabs, freshwater molluscs and mosquito larvae. In mid-June and possibly also in January, eggs measuring 30–31mm are laid. Restricted to Peninsular India.

## Narrow-headed Softshell Turtle *Chitra indica* 1.50m

A bizarre softshell turtle, its eyes are located very close to the snout. Head narrow; shell of juveniles with numerous small tubercles and a vertebral keel; dorsum dull olive or bluish grey, with a pattern of dark wavy reticulations, carapace pattern continuing up to neck and outer surface of forelimbs; a V-shaped mark commences on nape and extends to carapace; plastron cream or pale pink; head olive with dark-bordered, yellow streaks. Inhabits sandy sections of rivers and ambushes fish underwater by burying itself in sand, and also consumes molluscs. Nests laid between end-August and mid-September, in sandy or sandy-loam soils. Eggs brittle-shelled, spherical, 25–28mm, clutches containing 65–187 eggs. Incubation period 40–70 days, hatchlings 3.9–4.3cm. Isolated records from Peninsular India, and more widespread in northern India, besides Pakistan, Nepal and Bangladesh.

# Indian Flapshell Turtle *Lissemys punctata* 37cm

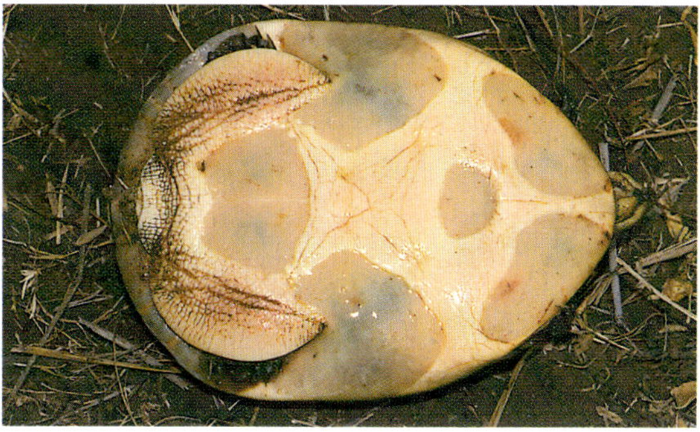

*Plastron*

A domed softshell turtle with plastral flaps. Shell oval, with hinged anterior lobe of cream or pale yellow plastron; a pair of flaps; carapace olive-green. Inhabits ponds, rivers, rice fields and canals. Scavenges on animal corpses far from water bodies; also takes tadpoles, fish, invertebrates and water plants. Egg-laying in northern India October–November, eggs nearly spherical, clutches 5–14 eggs, 24–30mm. The southern populations produce 2–8 eggs, 25–33mm. Incubation 9 months and hatchlings 4.2cm. Widespread in India, also Pakistan, Nepal, Sri Lanka, Bangladesh and northern Myanmar.

# Asian Giant Softshell Turtle *Pelochelys cantorii* 1.50m

The largest freshwater turtle in the region, inhabiting coastal areas. Shell low and depressed, elongated in young, oval in adults; juveniles showing numerous tubercles on carapace and a low vertebral keel; proboscis extremely short and rounded; carapace olive or brown, spotted or streaked with lighter or darker shades, with a lighter outer edge. Diet comprises fish, shrimps, crabs and molluscs and aquatic plants. Between 20–28 eggs laid at a time. Recorded from both coasts of India, the range including Bangladesh, Myanmar, Thailand, Peninsular Malaysia, Borneo, southern China and Vietnam.

# Glossary

**adult** Sexually mature individual.
**anterior** Nearer the front (towards head).
**aquatic** Species that live in water.
**arboreal** Species that live in trees or in other vegetation away from the ground.
**canopy** Layer of vegetation above ground, usually comprising tree branches and epiphytes.
**clutch** Total number of eggs laid by a female at a time.
**clutch size** Number of eggs in a nest.
**courtship** Behaviour preceding mating.
**crepuscular** Active during dawn and dusk.
**depressed** Flattened from top to bottom.
**diurnal** Active during the day.
**dorsal** The top or upper side of an animal, including the upper surfaces of the tail and limbs.
**dorsum** Dorsal surface of body, excluding head and tail.
**endemic** Restricted to a particular region.
**femoral pores** Pores present on femoral region of some geckos.
**fossorial** Species that live underground.
**infralabial** Scales on lower lip.
**keel** A narrow prominent ridge.
**lamella (pl. lamellae)** Pads under digits in lizards (also scansor).
**litter** Detritus of fallen leaves, branches and bark that accumulate on the forest floor.
**mid-dorsal** Scales around middle of body.
**nocturnal** Active during night.
**oviparous** Egg-laying.
**ovoviviparous** Form of reproduction when the eggs develop within the body of the mother, who does not provide nutrition other than the yolk.
**posterior** Nearer the back (towards tail).
**preanal pores** Pores situated in front of cloaca in geckos.
**prefrontals** Paired scales on anterior margin of orbit of eye, usually bounded by the frontal.
**recurved** Curved or bent.
**reticulate** Arranged like a net.
**scansor** Pads under digits in geckos (also lamella).
**scute** A horny epidermal shield.
**serrated** Possessing a saw-toothed edge.
**subcaudal** Scales below tail.
**supralabial** Scales on upper lip.
**tubercle** Knot-like projection.
**tympanum** Ear-drum.
**ventral** Scales under body, from throat to vent.
**vermiculation** Pattern consisting of vague, worm-like markings.
**vertebral** Pertaining to the region of the backbone.
**viviparous** Live-bearing, whereby the embryo obtains additional nourishment from the mother, in addition to the yolk.

# Further reading

Daniel, J. C. 1983. *The Book of Indian Reptiles*. Oxford University Press/Bombay Natural History Society, Bombay. 141 pp.

Das, I. 1995. *Turtles and Tortoises of India*. World Wide Fund for Nature – India/Oxford University Press, Bombay. x + 176 + (3) pp.

Das, I. 1996. *Biogeography of the Reptiles of South Asia*. Krieger Publishing Company, Malabar, Florida. 16 pl. + vii + 87 pp.

Das, I. 2001. *Die Schildkröten des Indischen Subkontinents*. Edition Chimaira, Frankfurt am Main. 160 pp.

Minton, S. A. 1966. A contribution to the herpetology of West Pakistan. *Bulletin of the American Museum of Natural History* 134: 27–184.

Rajendran, M. V. 1985. *Studies in Uropeltid Snakes*. Madurai Kamaraj University, Madurai. (4) + 132 pp.

Smith, M. A. 1931. *The Fauna of British India, including Ceylon and Burma. Vol. I. Loricata, Testudines*. Taylor and Francis, London. xxviii + 185 pp + 2 pl.

Smith, M. A. 1935. *The Fauna of British India, including Ceylon and Burma. Reptilia and Amphibia. Vol. II. Sauria*. Taylor and Francis, London. xiii + 440 pp + 1 pl.

Smith, M. A. 1943. *The Fauna of British India, Ceylon and Burma, including the whole of the Indo-Chinese region. Vol. III. Serpentes*. Taylor and Francis, London. xii + 583 pp + 1 map.

Whitaker, R. 1978. *Common Indian Snakes: a Field Guide*. Macmillan India Limited, New Delhi. xiv + 154 pp.

Zhao, E.-M. and K. Adler. 1993. *Herpetology of China*. Society for Study of Amphibians and Reptiles, Contributions to Herpetology, No. 10, Oxford, Ohio. 522 pp + 48 pl. + 1 folding map.

# Index

*Acanthodactylus cantoris* 103
Acrochordidae 12
*Acrochordus granulatus* 12
Agama, Caucasian 77
  Himalayan 77
  Lesser 69
Agamidae 69, 117
*Ahaetulla nasuta* 16
  *prasina* 17
*Amphiesma beddomei* 17
  *khasiense* 18
  *platyceps* 18
  *stolatum* 19
  *venningi* 19
*Amyda cartilaginea* 136
*Argyrogena fasciolatus* 20
*Asymblepharus ladacensis* 105
  *sikkimensis* 105
*Atretium schistosum* 20

*Batagur baska* 123
  *dhongoka* 126
  *kachuga* 127
Bataguridae 123
Bent-toed Gecko,
  Andaman 91
  Khasi Hills 90
  Lawder's 91
  Nicobar 90
Black Turtle, Indian 128
Black-headed Snake,
  Duméril's 45
  Collared 45
Blind Snake, Brahminy 57
  Jerdon's 58
  Large 58
*Blythia reticulata* 21
Boidae 13
*Boiga andamanensis* 21
  *ceylonensis* 22
  *dightoni* 22
  *forsteni* 23
  *multifasciata* 23
  *multomaculata* 24
  *nuchalis* 24
  *ochracea* 25
  *trigonata* 25
  *wallachi* 26
Box Turtle, Keeled 131
  Malayan 124
*Brachysaura minor* 69
*Bronchocela cristatella* 70
*Bufoniceps laungwalansis* 70
*Bungarus caeruleus* 50
  *fasciatus* 51
  *niger* 51

*Calliophis nigrescens* 52
*Calodactylodes aureus* 85
*Calotes calotes* 71
  *elliotti* 71
  *grandisquamis* 72
  *jerdoni* 72
  *nemoricola* 73
  *rouxii* 73

  *versicolor* 74
Cane Turtle, Cochin
  Forest 125
*Cantoria violacea* 26
*Caretta caretta* 131
Cat Skink, Beddome's 113
  Travancore 113
Cat Snake, Andamans 21
  Collared 24
  Common Indian 25
  Forsten's 23
  Many-banded 23
  Many-spotted 24
  Nicobarese 26
  Sri Lankan 22
  Tawny 25
  Travancore 22
*Cerberus rynchops* 27
*Chamaeleo zeylanicus* 82
Chamaeleon, South
  Asian 82
Chamaeleonidae 82
*Chelonia mydas* 132
Cheloniidae 131
*Chitra indica* 138
*Chrysopelea ornata* 27
*Cnemaspis assamensis* 86
  *indica* 86
  *littoralis* 87
  *nairi* 87
  *otai* 88
  *tropidogaster* 88
Cobra, Andaman 54
  Central Asian 54
  King 55
  Large-eyed False 43
  Monocled 53
  Spectacled 53
*Coelognathus flavolineatus* 28
  *helena* 32
  *radiatus* 28
Colubridae 16
Coral Snake, Black
  Slender 52
  MacClelland's 52
*Coronella brachyura* 29
*Coryphophylax subcristatus* 74
*Cosymbotus platyurus* 89
Crested Lizard, Green 70
Crocodile, Mugger 121
  Saltwater 122
Crocodylidae 121
*Crocodylus palustris* 121
  *porosus* 122
*Crossobamon orientalis* 89
*Cryptelytrops albolabris* 64
  *andersoni* 64
  *cantori* 65
  *gramineus* 65
  *malabaricus* 66
*Cuora mouhotii* 131
*Crytodactylus lawderanus* 91
*Cuora amboinensis* 124
*Cyclemys oldhami* 124
*Cyrtodactylus adleri* 90

  *khasiensis* 90
  *rubidus* 91
*Cyrtopodion kachhense* 92
  *scabrum* 92

*Daboia russelii* 60
*Dasia nicobarensis* 106
  *sia olivacea* 106
Day Gecko,
  Andaman 102
  Assamese 86
  Coastal 87
  Indian 86
  Ota's 88
  Ponmudi 87
  Rough-bellied 88
*Dendrelaphis cyanochloris* 29
  *grandoculis* 30
  *pictus* 30
  *tristis* 31
Dermochelyidae 133
*Dermochelys coriacea* 133
Dibamidae 83
*Dibamus nicobaricum* 83
*Draco blanfordi* 75
  *dussumieri* 75
Dravidogecko 96

*Echis carinatus* 61
*Elaphe frenata* 32
  *prasina* 33
Elapidae 50
*Enhydrina schistosus* 55
*Enhydris enhydris* 34
*Eretmochelys imbricata* 132
*Eryx conicus* 13
  *johnii* 14
  *whitakeri* 14
Eublepharidae 83
*Eublepharis fuscus* 84
  *macularius* 84
Eyed Turtle,
  Indian 128

Fan-throated Lizard 81
  Green 80
Flapshell Turtle,
  Indian 139
Flying Lizard,
  Blanford's 75
  Western Ghats 75
Flying Snake, Ornate 27
*Fordonia leucobalia* 34
Forest Lizard, Bay
  Islands 74
  Elliot's 71
  Green 71
  Jerdon's 72
  Large-scaled 72
  Nilgiri 73
  Roux's 73
Fringe-toed Lizard,
  Indian 103

Garden Lizard,
  Indian 74

Gavialiidae 122
*Gavialis gangeticus* 122
Gecko, Anaimalai 96
　Bark 99
　Bowring's 96
　Flat-tailed 89
　Four-clawed 94
　Garnot's 98
　Indian Golden 85
　Mourning 102
　Reticulated 100
　Sindh Sand 89
　Smith's Giant 95
　Termite-hill 100
　Tokay 95
*Geckoella collegalensis* 93
　*dekkanensis* 93
　*nebulosa* 93
*Gehyra mutilata* 94
*Gekko gecko* 95
　*smithii* 95
Gekkonidae 85
*Geochelone elegans* 134
*Geoclemys hamiltonii* 125
*Gerardia prevostiana* 35
Gharial 122
*Gloydius himalayanus* 61
*Gonyosoma oxycephalum* 35
Grass Skink, Andaman 108
　Bronze 109
　Four-keeled 110
　Keeled 109
　Lined 111
　Many-lined 110
　Rough-backed 111
　Tytler's 112
Ground Gecko,
　Clouded 94
　Deccan 93
　Kollegal 93
Ground Skink, Palni
　Hills 114
　Reeves's 115
　Side-spotted 114

*Hardella thurjii* 126
*Hemidactylus*
　*anamallensis* 96
　*bowringii* 96
　*brookii* 97
　*flaviviridis* 97
　*frenatus* 98
　*garnotii* 98
　*leschenaultii* 99
　*maculatus* 99
　*reticulatus* 100
　*triedrus* 100
*Hemiphyllodactylus*
　*aurantiacus* 101
　*typus* 101
Hill Turtle,
　Tricarinate 127
House Gecko, Asian 98
　Brooke's 97
　Yellow-green 97
Hydrophiidae 55
*Hydrophis cyanocinctus* 56

*Hypnale hypnale* 62
Indian Kangaroo
　Lizard 78
*Indotestudo elongata* 135
　*travancorica* 135
Iridescent Snake 21

*Japalura tricarinata* 76
　*variegata* 76

*Kaestlea laterimaculata* 114
　*palnium* 114
Keelback Water Snake,
　Andamans 47
　Checkered 48
　St John's 48
Keelback, Beddome's 17
　Buff-striped 19
　Eastern 18
　Günther's 18
　Himalayan 44
　Red-necked 44
　Venning's 19
　Yellow-spotted 47
Krait, Banded 51
　Black 51
　Indian 50
Kukri Snake,
　Banded 40
　Mandalay 41
　Spot-tailed 40
　Streaked 41
　White-barred 39

Lacerta, Leschenault's 104
　Snake-eyed 103
Lacertidae 103
*Laticauda colubrina* 56
*Laudakia caucasia* 77
　*himalayana* 77
　*tuberculata* 78
Leaf Turtle,
　Oldham's 124
Leopard Gecko,
　Common Asian 84
　Western Indian 84
*Lepidochelys olivacea* 133
*Lepidodactylus lugubris* 102
Leptotyphlopidae 57
*Leptotyphlops*
　*macrorhynchus* 57
*Liopeltis frenatus* 36
*Lipinia macrotympana* 107
*Lissemys punctata* 139
Litter Skink,
　Dussumier's 115
　Himalayan 116
　Spotted 116
Long-tailed Lizard,
　Khasi Hills 104
*Lycodon aulicus* 36
　*capucinus* 37
　*flavomaculatus* 37
　*jara* 37
　*striatus* 38
　*travancoricus* 39

*Lygosoma bowringii* 107
　*punctata* 108

*Mabuya andamanensis* 108
　*carinata* 109
　*macularia* 109
　*multifasciata* 110
　*quadricarinata* 110
　*rudis* 111
　*rugifera* 111
　*tytleri* 112
Mangrove Snake,
　White-bellied 34
　Yellow-banded 26
*Manouria emys* 136
Marsh Snake, Glossy 35
*Melanochelys*
　*tricarinata* 127
　*trijuga* 128
Monitor, Bengal 118
　Desert 119
　South-east Asian
　　Land 118
　Water 120
　Yellow 119
*Morenia petersi* 128
Mountain Lizard,
　Three-keeled 76
　Variegated 76

*Naja kaouthia* 53
　*naja* 53
　*oxiana* 54
　*sagittifera* 54
Narrow-headed Snake,
　Günther's 49
*Nilssonia gangeticus* 137
　*hurum* 137
　*leithii* 138

*Oligodon albocinctus* 39
　*arnensis* 40
　*dorsalis* 40
　*taeniolata* 41
　*theobaldi* 41
*Ophiomorus raithmai* 112
*Ophiophagus hannah* 55
*Ophisops jerdoni* 103
　*leschenaultii* 104
*Orthriophis cantoris* 31
　*hodgsonii* 33
*Otocryptis beddomii* 78
*Ovophis monticola* 62

*Pangshura smithii* 129
　*sylhetensis* 129
　*tectum* 130
　*tentoria* 130
*Pelochelys cantorii* 139
*Peltopelor macrolepis* 66
*Phelsuma andamanense* 102
*Phrynocephalus theobaldi* 79
Pit Viper, Anderson's 64
　Blotched 62
　Brown-spotted 63
　Cantor's 65
　Green 65

143

Himalayan 61
Hump-nosed 62
Jerdon's 63
Large-scaled 66
Malabar 66
Medo 67
Pope's 67
Stejneger's 68
White-lipped 64
*Platyplectrurus madurensis* 59
Pond Turtle, Spotted 125
pond turtles, Asian 123
*Popeia popeiorum* 67
*Protobothrops jerdoni* 63
*mucrosquamatus* 63
*Psammodynastes pulverulentus* 42
*Psammophilus dorsalis* 79
*Psammophis leithii* 42
*Pseudoxenodon macrops* 43
*Ptyas mucosa* 43
*Ptyctolaemus gularis* 80
*Python molurus* 15
*reticulatus* 15
Python, Indian Rock 15
Reticulated 15

Racer, Banded 20
*Ramphotyphlops braminus* 57
Rat Snake, Indian 43
*Rhabdophis himalayanus* 44
*subminiatus* 44
Ribbon Snake, Pakistani 42
*Ristella beddomii* 113
*travancorica* 113
River Turtle, Crowned 126
Rock Agama, Kashmiri 78
South Indian 79
Rock Gecko, Keeled 92
Spotted 99
Warty 92
Rock Skink, Ladakhi 105
Sikkimese 105
Roofed Turtle, Assam 129
Brown 129
Indian 130
Painted 127
Three-striped 126
Royal Snake, Black-headed 46

*Salea anamalayana* 80
*horsfieldi* 81
Sand Boa, Common 13
Red 14
Whitaker's 14
Sandfish, Indian 112
*palnica* 114
*reevesi* 115
Scincidae 105
Sea Snake, Annulated 56
Banded 56

Hook-nosed 55
Sea Turtle, Hawksbill 132
Leatherback 133
Loggerhead 131
Olive Ridley 133
Shieldtail, Ashambu 59
Large-scaled 60
Madurai 59
*Sibynophis collaris* 45
*subpunctatus* 45
*Sinomicrurus macclellandi* 52
*Sitana ponticeriana* 81
Skink, Small-eared Striped 107
Slender Snake, Darjeeling 46
Smooth Snake, Indian 29
Softshell Turtle, Asian Giant 139
Indian 137
Indian Peacock 137
Leith's 138
Malayan 136
Narrow-headed 138
*Spalerosophis atriceps* 46
*Sphenomorphus dussumieri* 115
*indicus* 116
*maculatus* 116
Spiny Lizard, Anaimalai 80
Horsfield's 81
Spiny-tailed Lizard, Hardwicke's 117
Star Tortoise, Indian 134
Stripe-necked Snake 36
Sunbeam Snake 68
Supple Skink, Bowring's 107
Spotted 108

*Takydromus khasiensis* 104
Tent Turtle, Indian 130
Terrapin, River 123
Testudinidae 134
Thread Snake, Large-beaked 57
Toad-headed Agama, Theobald's 79
Toad-headed Lizard, Laungwala 70
Tortoise, Asian Giant 136
Elongated 135
Travancore 135
tortoises, land 134
*Trachischium fuscum* 46
Tree Skink, Nicobarese 106
Olive 106
Tree Snake, Blue Bronzeback 29
Common Bronzeback 31
Large-eyed Bronzeback 30
Painted Bronzeback 30

Trinket Snake, Copper-headed 28
Eastern 31
Green 33
Himalayan 33
Indian 32
Khasi Hills 32
Red-tailed 28
Yellow-striped 28
Trionychidae 136
*Tropidophorus assamensis* 117
Turtle, Green 132
turtles, marine 131
Typhlopidae 57
*Typhlops diardii* 58
*jerdoni* 58

Uromastycidae 117
*Uromastyx hardwickii* 117
Uropeltidae 59
*Uropeltis liura* 59
*macrolepis* 60

Varanidae 118
*Varanus bengalensis* 118
*flavescens* 119
*griseus* 119
*nebulosus* 118
*salvator* 120
*Vijayachelys silvatica* 125
Vine Snake, Common 16
Oriental 17
Viper, Mock 42
Russell's 60
Saw-scaled 61
Viperidae 60
*Viridovipera medoensis* 67
*stejnegeri* 68

Wart Snake 12
Water Skink, North-eastern 117
Water Snake, Common Smooth 34
Dog-faced 27
Olive Keelback 20
Triangle-backed 49
Wolf Snake, Barred 38
Common 36
Island 37
Travancore 39
Yellow-speckled 38
Yellow-spotted 37
Worm Gecko, Oceanic 101
Western Ghats 101
Worm Lizard, Nicobarese 83

*Xenochrophis flavipunctatus* 47
*piscator* 48
*sanctijohannis* 48
*trianguligerus* 49
*tytleri* 47
Xenopeltidae 68
*Xenopeltis unicolor* 68
*Xylophis stenorhynchus* 49